The Official Harvard Student Agencies Bartending Course

"This is the most useful, most readable bartending guide I know of."
— *Liz Grant, bartender, Copperfield's (Boston)*

Also by Harvard Student Agencies, Inc.

Let's Go: The Budget Guide to Europe

Let's Go: The Budget Guide to the USA

*Let's Go: The Budget Guide to California
and the Pacific Northwest*

Let's Go: The Budget Guide to Britain and Ireland

Let's Go: The Budget Guide to France

Let's Go: The Budget Guide to Italy

*Let's Go: The Budget Guide to Spain,
Portugal and Morocco*

Let's Go: The Budget Guide to Greece

Let's Go: The Budget Guide to Israel and Egypt

THE
OFFICIAL
Harvard Student Agencies
BARTENDING COURSE

by Harvard Student
Agencies, Inc.
Ellen Macdonald, Editor

Illustrated by Franco Iudiciani

ST. MARTIN'S PRESS : NEW YORK

References in this book to brand names do not reflect
a preference for or sponsorship of the products involved
on the part of Harvard Student Agencies, Inc.

THE OFFICIAL HARVARD STUDENT AGENCIES BARTENDING COURSE. Copyright ©1984 by
Harvard Student Agencies, Inc. All rights reserved. Printed in the United States of America.
No part of this book may be used or reproduced in any manner whatsoever without written
permission except in the case of brief quotations embodied in critical articles or reviews. For
information, address St. Martin's Press, 175 Fifth Avenue, New York, N.Y. 10010.

Library of Congress Cataloging in Publication Data
Main entry under title:
The Official Harvard Student Agencies bartending course.
Includes index.
1. Bartending. 2. Alcoholic beverages. I. Macdonald, Ellen. II. Harvard Student Agencies.
TX951.O34   1984   681.8′74   83-24655
ISBN 0-312-58217-X

10   9   8   7   6

Contents

Acknowledgments

I am a Problem Drinkwriter. I'll admit it. It took the work of many generous and patient people to help me overcome this affliction and live to see the results.

A keg of gratitude and my first-born child go to Maura Gorman and Herman Llevat (they should live so long!). Every word in this book owes its existence to their constant barrage of wit, wisdom, advice, encouragement, and juicy gossip, which fortified me throughout *almost* every drought. As each deadline loomed up—and then rolled right over me—I could always count on Maura and Herman to grab my caffeine-trembling hands, pull me back on my feet (quite a task in itself), and reglue my fingers to the typewriter.

May I also propose a toast to all other HSAites, past and present, who contributed to this spirited endeavor. As a reformed Problem Drinkmaker, I credit my miraculous cure to the real authors of this book, the people at the Harvard Bartending Course and Harvard Catering: Chris Davis, Bill Coughlin, Claudio Phillips, Ross Pastel, Dave Mazza, Toni Brennan, Ed Salvato, Blanche Salvucci, and especially Narri Cooper for her editing. On the creative team, Franco Iudiciani deserves several medals for coming through with brilliant ideas and illustrations, despite my erratic direction. Thanks also to Brian Mullaney and Mike Ereli for their conception and interpretation of the Problem Drinkmaker theme. Of course, I wouldn't be where I'm not today were it not for the "bubbly" enthusiasm of Dan Del Vecchio, the inventor of this crazy scheme, and Hope Spruance, deft untangler of financial red tape. Ditto for Richard Milano, whose stamina and endurance in researching the "whiskey category" never ceased to amaze me. Above all, any remaining sanity I may possess at this writing I attribute solely to the extra-dry wit of Mary P. Keating. Her long, desk-side vigils made typing and other office inconveniences seem almost fun.

For more serious matters, I found it necessary to venture above ground—yes, into the *real* world. Fortunately, the kindness and generosity of several real-world people helped minimize the trauma. Paul Gorman and Arville Stephen of the Human Resource Institute contributed information and sensitivity to the side effects chapter; James Ryan and James Peters provided valuable consultation on alcohol-related legislation.

For Jared Kieling and Janet Vultee of St. Martin's Press, I can't think of the right words to express my gratitude . . . but that's okay, they're used to that. Besides, they'd probably just think up better ones anyway.

Finally, a very special thank you to the Quincy contingent: To Amy Badger for her dedication and professionalism throughout many a long night of research at Kelly's, and to my parents for donating the generous research grant . . . and then pretending not to notice when I felt the effects.

Introduction

Do your sloe gin fizzes fizzle out? Is your Golden Dream a frightening nightmare? Do you think rye is something you put mayonnaise on? Do your kegs produce enough foam to surf in? Try this simple quiz. Just answer yes or no in the blanks next to those questions that apply to you, and then tally up the responses. Be honest, now.

_____ Do you sometimes forget what you put in a drink the night before?
_____ Do you mix terrible drinks two, three, even four times a week?
_____ Do you ever lose control of your motor skills when mixing a cocktail?
_____ Do you ever mix awful drinks first thing in the morning?

If you answered yes to any of the above questions, it's time to admit what your friends and family have known for years: *You* are a Problem Drinkmaker. "No!" you might exclaim, "that happens to other people, not me." Don't be embarrassed and, above all, don't panic. It can happen to anybody. There is a cure, and it's rather fun and simple. Remember, though, the first step to getting better is admitting it. The second step is *The Official Harvard Student Agencies Bartending Course*.

You are one of the fortunate ones. For years, problem

drinkmaking was incurable. Millions of helpless Americans continued to pour foul-tasting cocktails, while researchers at the world's centers of learning worked fervently around the clock in search of the elusive cure. Finally, eleven years ago—a breakthrough! Eminent mixologists at Harvard Student Agencies established a unique, intensive bartending course offering therapy to those who could not mix on their own.

Today, the famous Harvard Bartending Course is the largest in New England, boasting over 25,000 successful and happy graduates. Now, thanks to these diligent social pioneers and their humanitarian efforts, Problem Drinkmakers nationwide can share in the secrets of the Harvard Bartending Correspondence Course with this book. Whether you aim to be a professional bartender, earn a little extra money part-time, mix drinks at cocktail parties, or just pour perfect gin and tonics for yourself, this book will teach you the basics for all types of bartending.

So relax. Take the cure slowly at first, because sometimes things get a little too much fun, too exciting for beginners to handle. Eventually, when *you* feel ready, try pouring yourself a beer, or maybe a glass of wine. Before you know it, especially with the support of your friends, you'll be mixing cocktails like a pro—and then you'll be cured. The best part is, the problem will never recur, and you can function fully in society as a normal human being for the rest of your life.

Cheers!

:1:

The First Step to Getting Better *Preparation*

If you are like most Problem Drinkmakers, that first step behind the bar can be a frightening experience. In some bars, you might face rows and rows of mysterious bottles, a confusing array of gadgets, utensils, and garnishes, and a strange assortment of glassware in every shape and size imaginable. Will it make you feel any better to know that many bartenders never even use most of those fancy bottles, tools, and glasses? In fact, bartending can be simple—and fun—once you get the hang of a few basics.

So, relax! Sit down, make yourself a drink (though maybe you'd better have someone else pour it for you now) and curl up with this good book. You won't even have to mix anything until chapter 2. Just try to become acquainted with the bar so mixing drinks will seem easier later on.

First, you'll need to know about:

- how all those bottles are usually arranged on the bar
- utensils you may need for mixing drinks
- different kinds of glasses you might find behind the bar
- garnishes and condiments you can use to enhance the taste and/or appearance of drinks
- terms and measurements experienced bartenders use

The Bars—Front and Back

If you've ever looked closely at a professional bar, or at a well-stocked one at home, you've probably noticed that bottles are generally kept in two main areas: the "front" bar and the "back" bar. A good bottle arrangement enables bartenders to make drinks efficiently, without having to search all over the place for the bottle they need next.

At the front bar, known also as the "cocktail party" bar or the "speed" bar, bartenders mix more than 70 percent of their drinks. In fact, many people who call themselves bartenders never get beyond the front bar. This might be easier than you thought! Imagine—you'll be able to call yourself a bartender, show off in front of friends, and hang up your framed Harvard "Master of Mixology" diploma (you'll find out how to obtain this diploma at the end of the book)—all without ever having to touch more than eight bottles!

As the names "cocktail party" and "speed" suggest, bartenders make gin and tonics and Scotch and waters at the front bar; all the basic, most popular drinks come from this area.

A typical front bar, cocktail party, or home bar setup looks like this:

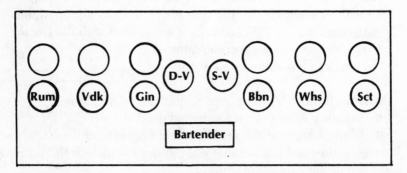

Front Bar Setup

Rum, vodka, and gin (Rum, Vdk, Gin)—the light alcohols—go on the left. (Often, tequila goes on the front bar with the lights as well.) On the right are bourbon, blended whiskey, and Scotch (Bbn, Whs, Sct)—the dark alcohols. In the middle, dry vermouth (D-V) and sweet vermouth (S-V). The dry vermouth stands next to the gin so you can quickly make a martini with the two, and the sweet vermouth is next to the bourbon so you can just as rapidly mix a Manhattan. The row of empty circles above represents the "show row." The show row, found on some cocktail, home, and front bars, is exactly the same as the row behind it, except that each bottle remains sealed and has the label facing the guests so they can read what brands the bartender pours.

Some bartenders prefer other setups at the front bar.

Here, the bartender chose to alternate light and dark alcohols and kept the vermouths to the side within easy reach. You can often design your own organization of the front

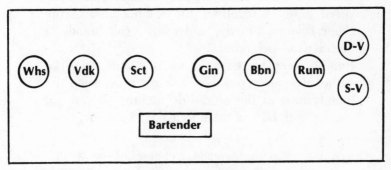

Alternate Front Bar Setup

bar, especially when working alone. The key is speed—set up the bottles so you can find them quickly and efficiently when you need to. (For more detailed diagrams, including garnish and mixer placement, see chapter 4, pages 107-12.)

In professional bars, a "speed rack" usually replaces the front bar. This rack, attached to the bar or sink directly in front of the bartender, holds "house brands" (usually less-

expensive brands) of front-bar liquor. The bartender pours
house liquor into every drink unless the customer specifies a
well-known brand; name brands, being more expensive, stay
on the back bar.

The back bar, also called the "liqueur" bar, contains liqueurs, brandies, "call" brands (those more expensive brands
of liquor requested by name), and other less frequently
ordered liquors. As the name suggests, bartenders usually
keep these bottles behind them, since they rarely have to use
these liquors and therefore don't mind walking a few extra
steps when they need to.

At first glance, the back bar appears to be a confusing array
of bottles, apparently thrown onto the shelves in random
order. Actually, the organization of the back bar follows two
basic, quite sensible rules:

> ***Rule 1:*** Keep bottles on the back bar separated by
> flavor base. For example, put the four orange-fla-
> vored liqueurs together, the Kahlua next to the
> coffee-flavored brandy, and all the call brands of
> Scotch near each other.
> ***Rule 2:*** Keep bottles used for the same drink to-
> gether whenever possible. For example, keep the
> brandy next to the crème de menthe so you can
> quickly grab both of them to make a stinger.

Of course, nobody expects a beginner or a Problem
Drinkmaker to name the four orange-flavored liqueurs, all
the call brands of Scotch, or the ingredients in a stinger.
Chapter 5 will take care of rule 1; it contains descriptions of
each liquor with liqueurs listed by flavor base.

As for rule 2, here are a few hints. In the center of the bar,
you'll probably find brandy with crème de menthe on its right
(as in a stinger) and crème de cacao on the left (as in a brandy
Alexander). Other possible combinations include: sloe gin
next to Southern Comfort (Sloe Comfortable Screw), tequila

next to triple sec (Margarita), and Cointreau in front of Galliano (Golden Dream).

Utensils

Bartenders usually keep a variety of tools around to help them do everything from pouring to shaking to straining. Here at Harvard, we call the most basic and useful utensils the "bartending kit"; most bartenders would never try to work without them. (To order your own official Harvard Bartending Kit, see page 204.) The kit contains:

>*Shaker set:* Bartenders use a shaker to make whiskey sours, daiquiris, Margaritas, and the other popular shaken drinks listed in chapter 3. We prefer a steel shell for the outer part and a glass shaker that fits inside. Glass works best for the inner part because some recipes call for you to "eyeball" the right amount of liquor in a drink; glass enables you to see how much you pour.

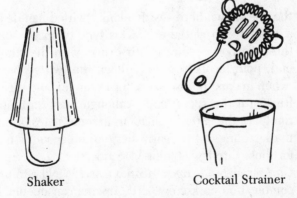

Shaker   Cocktail Strainer

>*Strainer:* The strainer fits over the shaker so you can pour a cold drink without letting the ice cubes fall into the glass ("straight up").

Speedpourers: Speedpourers fit into the mouth of a bottle and make the liquor come out at an even rate. As you will see in chapter 2, these gadgets are indispensable for the speed-oriented bartender. Make sure to put the speedpourer in the bottle at a right angle to the label; with all the pourers facing the same way, you can quickly grab each bottle without having to check the direction of the stream of liquor. Efficient!

Bar spoon: The bar spoon we recommend looks like

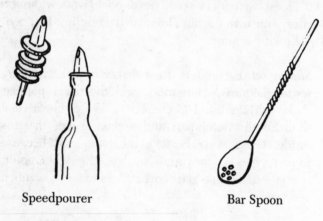

Speedpourer   Bar Spoon

the one shown here—with a long, twirled handle and a small spoon at the end. This type of spoon serves three purposes: you can stir drinks with the straight end, pour alcohol carefully down the twirled handle (when making pousse cafés, for example), and pick up fruit with the spoon end. Although busy bartenders rarely try the latter, regulations in some states prohibit the handling of fruit garnishes, so the spoon is made for those rare law-abiding bartenders.

Corkscrew/bottle opener/can opener: We like to use a combination corkscrew/bottle opener/can opener because three separate pieces can get lost too easily at a hectic bar. You should choose whatever feels most comfortable.

Corkscrew/Bottle Opener/
Can Opener   Shot/Measuring Glass

Shot glass/measuring glass: Although sometimes quite handy, a measuring glass is unnecessary when you have speedpourers. Some bars, however, insist that employees use measuring glasses to ensure that they don't pour too much and waste liquor.

You might decide to purchase any, all, or none of the utensils in the bartending kit, as well as some of the following:

Ice bucket: Bucket, basin, bag or whatever you have around for holding ice—anything clean is fine.
Ice tongs: Tongs enable the bartender to pick up ice without touching it. They are nice for some occasions, though impractical in a busy bar. Some states prohibit the bartender's handling ice . . . then again, some states prohibit eating peanuts on Sunday.
Knife: You will need a knife to cut up the fruit garnishes.

Glassware

The following list and illustrations will familiarize you with some glassware options available in bars. For the home, purchase any or all of them. In a professional establishment, the manager usually decides which glass to use for each drink. These illustrations are merely examples of different types; you'll find wide variations and creative adaptations from bar to bar. Be careful, though—don't be *too* creative. Remember, the right glass makes quite a difference in the final appearance of a drink— wine loses some of its appeal in a beer mug, and a piña colada won't fit in a shot glass.

> *Highball:* Used for more drinks than any other glass (for all those gin and tonics, Scotch and waters, etc.), highballs vary considerably from bar to bar. Most are clear, tall glasses that hold between 8 and 12 ounces.

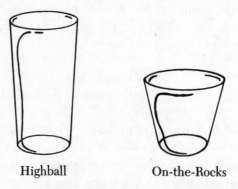

Highball   On-the-Rocks

On-the-rocks: Also used for many drinks, rocks or "lowball" glasses come in different shapes and designs. Most hold 4 to 9 ounces and are best for drinks served on the rocks—martini on the rocks, Scotch on the rocks, Black Russians, and many others.

Old Fashioned: This 4- to 7-ounce glass looks similar to an on-the-rocks glass, but has an indentation in the base to remind the bartender to prepare the sugar, water, and bitters mixture for an Old Fashioned. Today, many bars use these to do double duty as on-the-rocks glasses.

Collins: Best for Collinses, sloe gin fizzes, and

Old Fashioned

Collins

Singapore Slings, these 12-ounce glasses are frosted with some clear glass left at the top to remind the bartender to add soda water to the top of a Collins. They lend a cool, refreshing image to these drinks.

Whiskey sour: Sours are made by preparing the drink with ice, then straining it into this 4-ounce glass. If the glass were not stemmed, the sour would warm up quickly from the heat of the drinker's hand.

Whiskey Sour

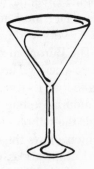

Cocktail

Cocktail: Drinkers often order martinis, Manhattans, and other cocktails "straight up," meaning, as with sours, that the drink is initially prepared with ice and then strained into this 4-ounce cocktail glass. The stem on the glass enables the drinker to hold the glass without warming up the chilled contents.

Wine: Wine glasses come in a very wide array of shapes and sizes. Choose yours according to your own preferences.

Wine   Sherry

Sherry: Serve sherry, port, or aperitifs like Dubonnet in these 2½- to 3½-ounce glasses.

Champagne: Champagne glasses come in two shapes and sizes. The American glass, by far the more popular here, is very wide and shallow and holds 4 to 6 ounces. The European glass, tall and fluted, has a 7- to 11-ounce capacity. The European glass is better for champagne than its American counterpart because the tapered mouth presents less surface area to the air and thus holds the bubbles in longer (unlike the American glass, which allows the bubbles to dissipate quickly). Also, the European glass causes fewer spilling problems.

Beer: Usually holding about 10 ounces, beer glasses come in two basic shapes: the mug and the Pilsner glass. Most people have already seen mugs. The Pilsner-style glass was invented for use with Pilsner beer (see chapter 5, page 151), but it is actually suitable for any kind. Bar managers often prefer mugs because they do not break as easily as the Pilsners.

American/European
Champagne

Mug/Pilsner Beer

Liqueur: Also known as a "pony," this 1-ounce glass is appropriate for after-dinner liqueurs and pousse-cafés.

Liqueur

Shot

Shot: These 1- to 2-ounce glasses can be used to serve shots of liquor or to measure alcohol.
Brandy: Brandy snifters range in capacity from 5 to 25 ounces. All have basically the same shape, and are designed to be cupped by the hand to warm the brandy.
Miscellaneous: You know the type—coconut shells in

Brandy Snifter

Miscellaneous

Polynesian restaurants, free tumblers from the gas station, oddball glasses lying around the house—anything that doesn't fit the above categories.

Garnishes, Garbage, Mixers, and Other Additives

Just as the right glassware can make a cocktail look infinitely more appealing, those additives the bartender puts in a drink also make it look—and, of course, taste—delicious. On the bar, you'll see colorful fruits; sweet, sparkling mixers; and a variety of other garnishes that add beauty and flavor to alcohol.

The words "garnish" and "garbage" refer to the fruits and vegetables you put in a drink. Although many bartenders use the two words interchangeably, technically they have different meanings. Garnishes *change the taste* of a drink, such as a lime wedge in a gin and tonic or a lemon twist in a bourbon. Garbage just makes the drink *look* pretty, such as a cherry in a Manhattan or an orange slice and pineapple chunk in a piña colada. Some garnishes and garbage often found on a bar are:

> *Oranges:* Slicing down through the stem, cut the orange in half. Lay each half on your cutting surface, flat slide down, and make semicircular, fanlike slices.

Make a little cut down the middle so that you can slide the slice over the rim of the glass—garbage never looked so lovely!

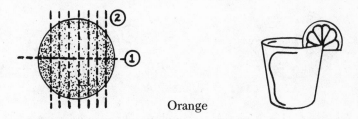

Orange

Lemons: Most drinkers prefer lemon *twists*, especially as a garnish in dark alcohols. To make twists, cut off the two ends of a lemon. With a spoon, force the fruit out one end and discard it. Slice the peel up as shown (you just use the peel in the drink). Twist the slice of peel, maybe rub it around the edge of the glass, drop it into the drink, and stir. It's also a good idea to keep some lemon slices or wedges at the bar, in case some fussy drinkers drop by who prefer a more lemony taste.

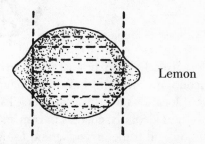

Lemon

Limes: Cut the lime in half (through its equator) and then quarter each half, following the natural contours of the fruit, to make eight wedges. Squeeze the lime over the drink, rub it around the edge of the glass if you like, and then drop it into the drink. Lime wedges are popular garnishes in many drinks, so keep plenty on hand. If you start to run low on limes, cut smaller wedges, but do *not* run out.

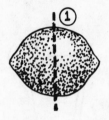

Lime

Cherries: Use stemmed maraschino cherries in your cocktails. Drinkers like stems so they can easily pull the cherry out of the drinks.

Olives: A must for the martini drinker, olives should be green, pitted, and without pimentos.

Onions: Get little cocktail onions for your Gibsons— Bermuda onions won't fit in the glass!

Cocktail Onion/Bermuda Onion

Bartenders usually keep at least four carbonated mixers up with the alcohol on the front bar. (The diagrams in chapter 4 show efficient locations for these mixers.) Two of these mixers go best with light alcohols: cola (as in rum and Coke) and tonic water (as in gin and tonic or vodka and tonic). The other two mix well with dark alcohols: soda water (as in Scotch and soda) and ginger ale (as in bourbon and ginger).

You might also want to have other carbonated mixers at the bar, such as 7-up or Sprite, bitter lemon, Collins mixer (although you'll read how to make Collinses from scratch in chapter 3), or any other of the many mixers available. Don't forget diet sodas; many people drink rum and diet cola, for example, to cut down on the extra calories, so keep that in mind as you stock mixers.

Some Problem Drinkmakers have trouble remembering the difference between soda water and tonic water; they use these two mixers interchangeably in drinks just because they look alike. Don't. Tonic contains sugar and bitter-tasting quinine. Soda water has bubbles in it, and sometimes a little salt—that's all. Some bars also serve Perrier, a naturally carbonated ("sparkling") spring water. If you plan to work at Ye Olde Sleazy Bar & Grille, however, seltzer (carbonated water) or soda water is fine.

Bottled mixers will suffice for the home bar or for a small, relaxed corner pub; soda taps work well in medium-sized, moderately busy bars; but when dealing with large, crowded, high-pressure establishments, only soda guns keep the mixer flowing fast enough. Also known as an "arm" or a "snake," this dispenser consists of a long, flexible tube with a set of buttons on the end. Each button represents a mixer; the bartender merely pushes a little button, and the desired soda gushes out of the gun. This device eliminates the inefficient hassle of searching all over the place for bottles, uncapping them, and running out every two minutes. If you work in a bar with a snake, ask the manager or a co-worker to show you how to set it up and make minor repairs.

Juices, of course, also go well with many liquors. Some popular mixing juices include orange, grapefruit, pineapple, cranberry, and tomato (some people prefer to buy a Bloody Mary mix instead of plain tomato juice).

Many drinks, such as Collinses, sours, and daiquiris, call for "sour" or "bar" mix. This mixer contains lemon juice, sugar, and some egg white to make the drinks slightly foamy. Sour mix often comes in powdered form (Quik-Lem, for example); in a pinch you could substitute frozen lemonade mixed with half the prescribed water.

Other mixers include:

Rose's lime juice: A sweetened, reconstituted lime juice used most often in gimlets. Rose's is sweetened, so do *not* substitute it in recipes calling for plain lime juice.

Cream: Don't use anything heavier than light cream or half-and-half, or you'll fill the drinker's stomach too quickly.

Milk: For sombreros, especially.

Water: To mix with whiskey . . . or Alka Seltzer, perhaps, if you're a real Problem Drinkmaker. If your bar does not dispense water through a tap or snake, keep water in a pitcher so all the air will dissipate. Otherwise, drinks will appear cloudy from the tiny air bubbles in tap water.

You'll find a wide variety of condiments and other mixings on a well-stocked bar. These include:

Sugar: Buy superfine granulated sugar, which mixes more easily in drinks and won't leave a syrupy layer on the bottom of the glass.

Simple syrup: As an alternative to dry sugar, some bartenders prefer to make simple syrup by mixing sugar and water together. Heat 1 pound of sugar in 1 quart of water until it dissolves. Keep a bottle on the bar with a speedpourer in it.

Salt: Keep a plate of salt on hand for making Salty Dogs and Margaritas.

Grenadine: This red, nonalcoholic sugar-and-pomegranate syrup colors and sweetens drinks.

Bitters: As the name suggests, this liquid is bitter and infrequently used in drinks these days. Sometimes you can add it to Manhattans or Bloody Marys if you like; always put some bitters in Old Fashioneds.

Bloody Mary mixings: Keep any or all of the following on hand for Bloodies: Tabasco sauce, Worcestershire sauce, salt and pepper, horseradish, celery stalks.

Nutmeg: For brandy Alexanders and eggnogs.

And, of course, the most important additive—*ice* (lots of it).

This rather extensive list of garnishes, mixers, and condiments should give you an idea of the kinds of additives to expect in chapter 3. Don't run out to the store and buy every one of them though; just pick and choose according to your preferences.

Terminology

Bartenders (and drinkers) love to throw around some terms that sound confusing at first but are actually quite simple once you've heard them a few times. Some of the words on the following list are important and helpful for communicating exactly what you want to order or mix.

Dash/splash: This refers to the amount of something in a drink, such as a dash of Tabasco sauce or a splash of water. Technically, a dash equals 1/6 teaspoon (a squirt) and a splash equals 1/2 ounce (a longer squirt), but a bartender very rarely measures these small amounts.

Shot: Shot has no precise definition, but usually ranges from 1 to 2 ounces depending on the bar and the size of its shot glasses.

Jigger: Measures 1½ ounces.

Pony: One ounce; also refers to a pony glass.

Nip: Nips are little bottles of liquor, popular as gifts at holiday time and as drink servings on airplanes (where they are also called *miniatures*). They come in three sizes: 1-ounce, 1.6-ounce, and 2-ounce.

Fifth: The traditional size of the American liquor bottle, now largely superseded by the 750 ml bottle; 1/5 gallon = 4/5 quart = 25.6 ounces.

Proof: Twice the percentage of alcohol. For example, 100 proof equals 50 percent alcohol. This term indicates the strength of the liquor.

Grain neutral spirits (GNS): This 190-proof (95 percent pure) alcohol has no distinctive color, odor, or taste. Both vodka and gin are initially prepared as GNS and then later filtered or flavored, and cut with distilled water. In some states it is possible to buy grain in liquor stores, but *be careful*—one grain drink would be as intoxicating as three to four ordinary drinks, yet *no* flavor, color, or odor signals this potency to the drinkers. GNS is very irritating to the throat and should never be drunk straight.

Neat: Alcohol served right from the bottle with no ice.

Straight up: A drink mixed in a glass with ice and then strained into another glass without ice (sometimes referred to as a "chilled" drink).

On the rocks: Refers to a drink with ice. In some cases, the drink is prepared as a straight-up drink, but is then strained into a glass with ice.

Side, Back, or Chaser: Some bars, instead of regular highballs, serve a glass of mixer with 1½ ounces of liquor on the side in a shot glass. This glass of mixer is called a side, back, or chaser.

Mist/frappé: Both terms refer to a drink served over shaved ice, but a mist is generally served in a rocks glass and a frappé in a cocktail or champagne glass. For example, a "crème de menthe mist" describes crème de menthe poured over shaved ice in a rocks glass.

Dry/wet: Refers to the proportion of vermouth in a martini, and to the kind of vermouth in a Manhattan. (For more information, see chapter 3, pages 45-47.)

Straight/blended: These terms refer to whiskey. (For more information, see chapter 5, pages 135-38.)

Labeling: Letters on a brandy or whiskey bottle stand

for very simple words. They are usually listed in combination with each other. For example, VSOP on a brandy label stands for Very Special Old Pale.

E	especially		C	cognac or Canadian
F	fine		Q	quart
M	mellow		S	special (or "superior")
V	very		P	pale
X	extra		O	old

Keg: (technically, a half-keg.) A stainless steel beer barrel holding 15.5 gallons.

Virgin: A drink prepared without the liquor.

Measurements: Most distillers and winemakers now use metric measurements. This chart will help you understand the relationship between standard and metric amounts.

Standard	Metric
1 pint = 16 oz	500 ml = 16.9 oz
1 fifth = 25.6 oz	750 ml = 25.4 oz
1 quart = 32 oz	1 liter = 33.8 oz

Other standard bottles are the *magnum* (52 ounces), the *jeroboam* (104 ounces), the *rehoboam* (156 ounces), and the *jeromagnum* (208 ounces). (It is probably okay to remember these last four terms as "a lot of liquor" or "very big bottles.")

There you have it! That first step behind the bar wasn't so bad after all! Now, with the help of that drink you had at the beginning of chapter 1, you're probably feeling more relaxed and confident about your bartending abilities. You know your way around the bar, feel comfortable with all the bottles, glasses, garnishes, and gadgets, so now you're ready for the *real* stuff. Keep reading—you're about to take the cure.

:2:

On the Road to Recovery
Mixing Drinks

Did you know that, despite the thousands of drink recipes listed in all those bartending books, there are only *three* basic types of drinks? Of course, if you want to talk about blenders and flames and other funny devices, you're opening a whole new can of worms, but most cocktails spring from variations on three simple techniques: highballs, stirred drinks, and shaken cocktails.

In this chapter, you'll proceed step by step through these three mixing techniques. You may be surprised, perhaps even a bit disillusioned, when you realize how simple bartending really is, but at least by the end of chapter 2, *nobody* can get away with calling you a Problem Drinkmaker ever again.

Highballs

Gin and tonic, Scotch and soda, rum and Coke, screwdriver . . . sound familiar? These drinks are highballs, which comprise at least 70 percent of all drinks a typical bartender serves. When you finish reading this short section on how to make a highball, you will have conquered 70 percent of all drinks! (Recipes are in chapter 3.) Some highballs require a little extra effort, but most are incredibly simple once you know the basic technique.

A highball usually measures about 9 ounces, including ice,

liquor, and mix. Serve it in (simply enough) a highball glass. Follow these steps:

1. Get a highball glass.
2. Fill the glass two-thirds full with ice.
3. Pour in one jigger (1½ ounces) of liquor.
4. Pour mixer in almost to the top. If you pour in too much, the drink will spill, but too little mixer looks chintzy.
5. If the mixer is noncarbonated, stir it, or stick a straw in and let the drinker stir it. With carbonated mixers, do not stir; the bubbles do the mixing, and stirring tends to make the carbonation go flat.
6. Garnish the drink, if necessary.

As mentioned in step 3, you must pour 1½ ounces of liquor into the drink. (Some bars prefer to save money by serving only 1-ounce highballs.) You can measure three ways; the Harvard Bartending Course follows method 3.

> *Method 1:* Pour liquor into the jigger glass to measure it, and then pour jigger into the drink. This method is accurate, but too slow and cumbersome if you're working at a crowded bar.
>
> Some bar managers insist that their employees use this method to ensure that no liquor is wasted. If you must follow this procedure some day, here's a way to pour faster and make customers think they're getting a stronger drink. First, hold the jigger glass in one hand and the liquor bottle in the other. Pour *less than* 1½ ounces of liquor into the jigger, and then dump that into the highball glass *while still pouring* a little more liquor from the bottle. To the customers, it appears as though you gave them a full jigger plus another splash from the bottle in each drink.
>
> *Method 2:* Bartenders call this method the "two

fingers" technique. Put your first two fingers together around the bottom of the glass and then pour in liquor until it reaches the top of your fingers. This method is faster than the jigger glass routine, but inaccurate; bartenders with bony fingers serve boring drinks, while ones with fat fingers get people drunk pretty quickly!

Method 3: Fast, accurate . . . it's the "four-count" technique. Do you remember reading about speed-pourers and how they fit into the mouth of a bottle to make the liquor come out at an even rate (see page 6)? With a speedpourer in, if you grab the liquor bottle by the neck, tip it completely upside down over the glass, and count to four at the right speed, you can measure out exactly 1½ ounces. (The Harvard Bartending Course pours a four-count, but you can use your own lucky number if you prefer.) Just get a bottle of colored water, put a speedpourer in it, and keep practicing until you get a cadence that measures exactly 1½ ounces. With enough practice, you won't even have to count anymore, but will pour the right amount automatically; a four-count will eventually *feel* right to you.

Remember, though, you must grab the bottle firmly by the neck to get the best leverage and control. You must also make sure to tip the bottle completely upside down so the right amount of alcohol comes out. Practice a few times until you get it right.

To review, here's how to make a gin and tonic:

1. Get a highball glass.
2. Reach into the ice bucket and grab some ice; fill the glass two-thirds full with it.
3. Grab the gin bottle by the neck for control and leverage.

4. Tip the bottle upside down and count to four (or whatever cadence you have developed).

5. Add tonic water. Fill the glass almost to the top to make it look full, but not overflowing. Don't stir—no need to stir carbonated mixers.

6. Squeeze a lime wedge over the top of the drink and drop it in.

Pretty easy, huh? Even *you* could do it! Now that you've learned 70 percent of the drinks, try your hand at stirred cocktails.

Stirred Cocktails

The stirred cocktail category includes drinks such as martinis, Manhattans, and gimlets. They are stronger than highballs and measure about 3 ounces of liquid.

You can make stirred cocktails two ways: straight up (or just "up") and on the rocks (or just "rocks"). Straight-up cocktails are made in a shaker glass with ice and then transferred to a cocktail glass without ice. On-the-rocks drinks can be made either right in a rocks glass with ice, or stirred in a shaker and transferred to a glass with fresh ice.

Practice here by making a martini up, and a gimlet on the rocks.

The martini recipe calls for about eight parts gin to one part dry vermouth.

1. Put ice in your shaker glass two-thirds of the way full.
2. Start with the ingredient you'll be using least of. Here, that is dry vermouth. Remember that a stirred cocktail should contain about 3 ounces of liquid, so one-ninth of that is only a little splash of dry vermouth.
3. Gin makes up the balance of the drink. Put in about a six-count (melting ice after stirring brings the liquid content up to 3 ounces).
4. Stir *well*. Stir it *really well*. Remember, this drink has to stay cold and this is the only time it will have ice in it. Stir with the straight end of your bar spoon so you won't spill ice cubes all over the place.
5. Strain the drink into a cocktail glass (or whatever glass you've chosen to serve it in). Put your strainer over the shaker glass and pour.
6. Garnish the martini with an olive.

You'll read more in chapter 3 about martini variations—"dry" martinis, for example. For now, go on to make a vodka gimlet on the rocks, which contains five parts vodka to one part Rose's lime juice.

1. Fill your shaker glass two-thirds full with ice.
2. Put in a long one-count of Rose's lime juice.
3. Pour in five times as much vodka as this. Eyeball it—hold the shaker glass in front of you as you pour and judge by sight how much to put in.
4. Stir, stir, stir . . .
5. Put strainer over the glass, and strain the drink into an on-the-rocks glass full of *fresh* ice.
6. If you wish, drop in a lime wedge as a pretty garnish.

Shaken Cocktails

This is the part of bartending that is fun and very professional-looking once you get the hang of it. You might forget a few steps at first and spill daiquiri all over yourself, but keep practicing.

Try to make a whiskey sour. The recipe calls for 2 ounces of blended whiskey, the juice of one-half lemon, and 1 teaspoon of sugar. But if you use a premixed *bar mix* or *sour mix* (see page 56), you will already have the lemon and sugar mixture made and bottled on your bar. Follow these steps for a whiskey sour:

1. Fill the shaker glass two-thirds full with ice.
2. Pour in 2 ounces blended whiskey—about a six-count.
3. Now pour in about 1–1½ ounces sour mix (depending on the sweetness of the mix and your preferences)—a three- or four-count.
4. Put the stainless steel shell over the shaker glass (as shown) and give the top a little tap to make a seal between the two. The steel shell is going to contract when the ice makes it cold, so the seal will get even stronger.
5. Hold the top and bottom of the shaker and shake it up and down. Eventually you can get fancy in your shaking, but always make sure the ingredients go up and down in the glass.

Step 4

Step 5

6. While you were shaking, the ice made the steel shell contract to form a stronger seal over the glass. You will have to break that seal now. Look for the frost line on the shell which indicates where the seal is, and then tap the

steel shell with the heel of your hand at that frost line. The seal makes a loud snap as it breaks, and the steel shell comes loose.

7. Keeping the shaker together, turn the *whole thing* over.

Step 6

Step 7

8. Separate: Take the glass out of the steel shell. (By turning the shaker over *before* separating the glass from the shell, you avoid making a mess; all the dribbles from the glass land *in* the shaker, not *on* the bar. Try taking the shell off without turning the unit over and you'll find yourself and the bar drenched in whiskey sour.)

9. Put the strainer over the shaker shell, and strain the drink into a whiskey sour glass or some other kind of lowball glass (preferably one with a stem, so that the drink will stay cold longer).

10. Garnish with a cherry and an orange slice.

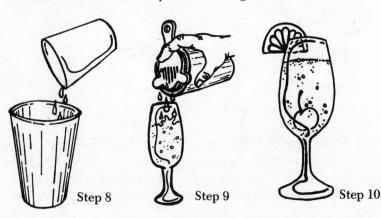
Step 8   Step 9   Step 10

11. Clean the shaker: Pour in some water, shake it around, dump it out, and then wipe the inside. Some shaken cocktails have milk or cream in them, in which case take special pains in cleaning the shaker—nobody likes a whiskey sour with little pieces of curdled milk adrift in it.

In review, here's how to put all those steps together to make a whiskey sour.

1. Fill shaker glass two-thirds full with ice.
2. Put in a six-count of blended whiskey.
3. Put in a three- or four-count of sour mix.
4. Place the stainless steel shell over the shaker glass and give the top a little tap to seal it in place.
5. Hold the top and bottom of the shaker and shake it up and down.
6. Tap the frost line of the steel shell with the heel of your hand to break the seal.
7. Turn the whole thing over so now the steel shell is on the bottom.
8. Lift out the shaker glass.
9. Strain the drink into a whiskey sour glass (or whatever glass you prefer).
10. Garnish with a cherry and an orange slice.
11. Clean the shaker.

Practice. Then practice some more. And then some more. If you don't like the recipes described here, try any or all of the ones listed in chapter 3.

Too much practice *does* create a couple of problems, though: poverty and drunkenness. If you tried to mix all the recipes in chapter 3, you'd go broke from buying all that liquor, and then you'd stagger and slur for a year after drinking all those trial runs.

Instead, take a few empty liquor bottles, fill them with colored water, and put speedpourers in them. First, practice pouring a perfect 1½-ounce four-count until you feel comfortable with it. Then run through the instructions in this chapter as well as a few recipes in chapter 3.

If you plan to work professionally some day, try this advanced technique. Line up some glasses on the bar or in the palm of your hand and "mass produce" two or three highballs. Real bartenders in a busy bar would never waste time making three gin and tonics separately, but would instead:

1. Put three ice-filled glasses close together on the bar.
2. Tip the bottle over the first glass for a four-count, and then just *move the bottle quickly over* to the second glass and then the third, before returning the bottle to an upright position.
3. Pour tonic in the three glasses.
4. Squeeze limes into the drinks.

Don't bother learning this method unless you plan on speed-bartending some day. Next time you go to a bar, watch the bartender and you'll learn other professional hints.

Most importantly, have *fun* tending bar. Mixing instructions in some bar books read like the training manual for a nuclear engineer's job. You're just mixing a drink. Of course, you can't substitute whiskey for water or vodka for vermouth, but on the other hand, the world will not end tomorrow if you pour 2 ounces instead of 1½. As evidence of this, notice how often recipes for the same drink differ from one bar book to another, and from one bar to the next. (If you skim through this chapter again, you'll see how many times the words "approximately," "about," "sort of," "nearly," and "vary according to your own preferences" pop up.)

So . . . stop a moment and pat yourself on the back. If you survived this chapter without hurting anybody or spilling too much, you are no longer a Problem Drinkmaker. Well, maybe you have a few problems left, but what follows will clear those up in no time. So forge onward and upward to the next hurdle—recipes.

:3:

Popular Prescriptions
Recipes

S ome bartending books boast in huge letters on the
cover, "Contains All the Drinks Ever Invented! Over
72 Million Recipes." Be serious. Who needs to (or wants to)
know even 72 *dozen* drink recipes? Even more important,
who in their right mind would really drink some of those
obscure, mysterious mixtures? Many of them haven't been
ordered since before Prohibition.

The Harvard Bartending Course prides itself on its
discriminating tastes. Only the most popular prescriptions for
the Problem Drinkmaker appear in this book—not just any
old concoction dredged up from the distant past. Flips?
Sangarees? Look somewhere else for those dinosaurs. Here
you'll find the standards, those favorites that people ask for
regularly. Of course, all the classics are in here, too; they're
not ordered in a bar as often as the favorites, but a good
bartender knows about them in case someone asks. And
adventurous types will love the novelty drinks scattered
throughout the chapter.

How to Use the Recipe Guide

Most of these recipes are categorized according to how they're
made. This setup enables you to learn and remember how to

make the drinks at the same time that you see the actual recipes. Unlike alphabetical listings (use the index to look up a recipe that way), this setup allows you to see what drinks are really just variations of others.

Each of the first three sections contains three subgroups: basics, populars, and funs. *Basic* drinks are the old stand-bys, such as gin and tonics in the highball section, martinis in the stirred section, and daiquiris in the shaken section. *Popular* drinks aren't quite as classic, but do require memorization if you plan to work in a bar someday. *Fun* drinks include many you've never heard of before and may never need again, so you only have to memorize the ones you like. Fun drinks are arranged alphabetically.

The twelve categories of drinks are:

   I. Highballs
     A. Basic (to memorize)
     B. Popular (to memorize if you plan to work in a bar)
     C. Fun drinks (don't memorize—arranged alphabetically)
  II. Stirred Cocktails
     A. Basic (to memorize)
     B. Popular (to memorize if you plan to work in a bar)
     C. Fun drinks (don't memorize—arranged alphabetically)
 III. Shaken Drinks
     A. Basic (to memorize)
     B. Popular (to memorize if you plan to work in a bar)
     C. Fun drinks (don't memorize—arranged alphabetically)
  IV. Blended Drinks
   V. Hot Drinks
  VI. Flame Drinks
 VII. Pousse-Cafés
VIII. Wine and Champagne Drinks
  IX. Coolers
   X. Beer Drinks

XI. Shots
XII. Punch Recipes (see chapter 4, page 112.)

: I. HIGHBALLS :

Serve the following drinks in highball glasses, unless you prefer another, more creative presentation. In case you've already forgotten how to make highballs, here's a quick refresher:

1. Get a highball glass.
2. Put ice in the glass two-thirds full.
3. Pour in 1½ ounces liquor—a four-count.
4. Fill almost to the top with mixer.
5. If the mixer is noncarbonated, stir the drink.
6. Garnish, if necessary.

A. Basic Highballs

These recipes are the most common ones you will serve, whether in a bar or at home. Memorize them—it's easy. They are arranged by liquor, in order to help you remember the ingredients.

GIN

Gin and Tonic
 1½ oz. gin
 tonic to fill
Garnish with a lime wedge.

Gin Chiller
    1½ oz. gin
    ginger ale to fill
Garnish with a lime wedge. Drinks with the name "chiller" contain ginger ale as a main ingredient.

Gin Rickey
    1½ oz. gin
    soda water to fill
Garnish with a lemon twist. This is the only gin-and-clear mixer drink garnished with a lemon twist—most call for a lime wedge.

Orange Blossom
    1½ oz. gin
    orange juice to fill
This drink is in fact a screwdriver with gin instead of vodka.

Tom Collins
    1½ oz. gin
    Collins mix to fill
Garnish with a cherry and an orange slice. (You'll find a better recipe for Collinses in the Shaken Drinks section, on page 58.)

Gin and Grapefruit Juice
    1½ oz. gin
    grapefruit juice to fill

Gin Fizz
    1½ oz. gin
    7-up or Sprite to fill
Garnish with a lime wedge.

VODKA

Vodka and Tonic
  1½ oz. vodka
  tonic water to fill
Garnish with a lime wedge.

Vodka Chiller
  1½ oz. vodka
  ginger ale to fill
Garnish with a lime wedge. Chiller drinks contain ginger ale.

Screwdriver
  1½ oz. vodka
  orange juice to fill

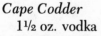

Cape Codder
  1½ oz. vodka
  cranberry juice to fill
Garnish with lime wedge. Here's an example of how to memorize drink recipes. If you can't remember that cranberries grow on Cape Cod, Massachusetts, try to remember all those Cs: Cape Codder and cranberry juice. Learn to associate and play word games like this one so you'll have an easier time recalling ingredients and proportions when you're tending bar.

Madras
  1½ oz. vodka
  orange juice to ¾ fill
  cranberry juice
Dribble cranberry juice around the top to give a mottled appearance. *Don't* stir. This drink should remind you of a bright, *madras* plaid.

Sea Breeze
   1½ oz. vodka
   grapefruit juice to ¾ fill
   cranberry juice to fill
Stir. This drink is a pretty pink color.

Salty Dog
   1½ oz. vodka
   grapefruit juice to fill
Pour this drink into a highball glass rimmed with salt. To rim a
glass with salt:

1. Pour salt on a plate.
2. Rub a lime wedge around rim of glass.
3. Roll rim of glass around in salt.

Remember—rim the glass with salt *before* you put the ice in it!

Greyhound
A Salty Dog without the salt.

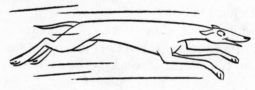

Vodka Collins
   1½ oz. vodka
   Collins mix to fill
Garnish with cherry and an orange slice. (You'll find a better
recipe for Collinses in the Shaken Drinks section, on page
58.)

Vodka and 7-up, Sprite, or Fruit Soda
   1½ oz. vodka
   7-up, Sprite, or any fruit soda to fill
Garnish with a cherry and an orange slice.

Bloody Mary
 1½ oz. vodka
 tomato juice to ¾ fill
 small splash lemon juice (or garnish with lemon slice or
  lime wedge)
 dash Worcestershire sauce
 dash Tabasco sauce (more for a hotter drink)
 shake of salt and pepper
 ¼ tsp. horseradish (optional)
Garnish with celery stick. "Bloody" drinkers have diverse
tastes, so you should ask the drinker if he or she would like
the drink hot, and then alter accordingly with Tabasco sauce.

Virgin Mary
A Bloody Mary without the vodka.

RUM

Rum and Tonic
 1½ oz. rum
 tonic water to fill
Garnish with lime wedge.

Rum and Cola
 1½ oz. rum
 cola (or diet cola) to fill

Cuba Libre
 1½ oz. rum
 cola to fill
Garnish with lime wedge. Cuba Libre ("free Cuba") is just a
fancy name for a rum and cola with a lime wedge.

Rum Chiller
 1½ oz. rum
 ginger ale to fill
Garnish with lime wedge. Chiller drinks contain ginger ale.

Rum Collins
    1½ oz. rum
    Collins mix to fill
Garnish with a cherry and an orange slice. (You'll find a better recipe for Collinses in the Shaken Drinks section, on page 58.)

Rum and Orange Juice
    1½ oz. rum
    orange juice to fill
Sometimes called a rum screwdriver.

Rum and Pineapple Juice
    1½ oz. rum
    pineapple juice to fill

Rum and 7-up, Sprite, or Fruit Soda
    1½ oz. rum
    7-up, Sprite, or fruit soda to fill
Garnish with lime wedge.

WHISKEY

The following highballs can contain bourbon, blended whiskey, Scotch, or some other whiskey. The drinker will tell the bartender what to put in; for example, Scotch and water. Often with these dark alcohols, drinkers prefer to choose a brand also; for example, a Dewar's and soda instead of just Scotch and soda.

Rye and ginger (or something like that) is another common request. You'll find a rye whiskey on many back bars (such brands as Old Overholt) if you look hard enough for it, but few people drink rye these days. The drinker probably wants *blended* whiskey (often referred to as "rye") and ginger. To obtain real rye, a person has to say "I want *real* rye, not blended whiskey."

Dealing with all the different kinds of whiskies often frustrates and confuses a Problem Drinkmaker, or a drinker of light alcohols, for that matter. If you fit into either one of these categories, read over the whiskey section of chapter 5 before trying to serve these drinks.

Whiskey and Water
1½ oz. whiskey
water to fill

Garnish with lemon twist. Some people request only a splash of water. A splash equals ½ ounce, so just put a little water in (don't measure out ½ ounce) and serve it in a rocks glass.

Whiskey and Soda
1½ oz. whiskey
soda to fill

Garnish with lemon twist.

Whiskey and Ginger
1½ oz. whiskey
ginger ale to fill

Some drinkers call this a "highball."

Presbyterian
1½ oz. whiskey (usually blended)
equal parts soda water and ginger ale to fill

This drink is often called a "Press" or a "VO Press." The latter contains Seagrams VO whiskey, a name brand. If you don't have VO, suggest another blended whiskey as a substitute (such as Canadian Club).

John Collins
1½ oz. whiskey
Collins mix to fill

Garnish with a cherry and an orange slice (You'll find a better recipe for Collinses in the Shaken Drinks section, on page 58.)

Seven and Seven
   1½ oz. Seagram's 7
   7-up to fill
This drink requires name-brand whiskey and the right mixer.
If you don't have one or either, suggest substitutes, such as
VO and ginger. Make sure to tell the drinker when you must
substitute ingredients.

Some whiskey drinkers want nothing to do with mixers.
They'll order a Scotch on the rocks or blended whiskey with
just a splash of water. Some will request a brand, such as
"J&B neat" (neat means no ice—pour it right from the bottle).
Serve these drinks in rocks glasses.
   The garnish for dark alcohols is usually a lemon twist, both
for lowballs (rocks) and highballs. With sweet mixers, leave
out the twist.

BRANDY AND LIQUEURS

_____ *and Soda*
   1½ oz. brandy, or liqueur, or aromatic wine
   soda to fill
Some examples of common liqueurs to mix with soda are:
Kahlúa, amaretto, Midori, crème de menthe, Campari, and
fruit-flavored brandies. Aromatics are wines fortified with
brandy and other ingredients; examples include vermouth
and Dubonnet.

_____ *Chiller*
   1½ oz. brandy, liqueur, or aromatic wine
   ginger ale to fill
Examples: mint chiller (crème de menthe), Dubonnet chiller,
Comfort chiller (Southern Comfort).

B. Popular Highballs

The popular-drink section contains recipes that are either simple variations on the basics, or more complicated yet often-ordered drinks. If you plan to work at a bar, memorize these recipes. They are arranged by liquor type (and, within these, by variations) to make it easier for you to remember ingredients and proportions.

To make these popular highballs, follow these steps:

1. Get a highball glass.
2. Fill two-thirds full with ice.
3. Put the liquors in first.
4. Add mixers as described in the recipe.
5. Stir, if noncarbonated.
6. Garnish, if necessary.

Vodka and Apple Juice (or Lemonade)
1½ oz. vodka
apple juice or lemonade to fill

Downeaster
1½ oz. vodka
equal amounts of pineapple juice and cranberry juice to fill

Moscow Mule
2 oz. vodka
ginger beer to fill
Garnish with lime wedge. Traditionally served in a copper mug.

Harvey Wallbanger
1½ oz. vodka
orange juice (fill almost to top)
1 oz. Galliano (float on top)
This is just a screwdriver with Galliano on top.

Orange Chiller
    1½ oz. gin (or other liquor)
    ginger ale to ¾ fill
    orange juice to fill
This is just a gin chiller (or other chiller) with some orange juice in it.

Rum Cape Codder
    1½ oz. rum
    cranberry juice to fill
Just substitute rum for vodka in a Cape Codder.

Oogie Pringle
    1½ oz. rum
    pineapple juice and cranberry juice to fill
This is just a Downeaster with rum instead of vodka.

Tequila Sunrise
    1½ oz. tequila
    orange juice to fill
    splash (½ oz.) of grenadine
Make this like a "tequila screwdriver" and stir; then add the grenadine and *do not stir* (not stirring achieves the sunrise look).

Claudio's Tequola
    1½ oz. tequila
    cola to fill
Garnish with lime wedge. This is just like a tequila version of the Cuba Libre. Drinkers call this by other names, such as tequila and cola.

Bloody Maria
    1½ oz. tequila
    tomato juice to ¾ fill
    small splash lemon juice (or garnish with lemon slice or
        lime wedge)

dash Worcestershire sauce
dash Tabasco sauce (more for hot drink)
a shake of salt and pepper
1/4 tsp. horseradish (optional)
Garnish with celery stalk. Ask the drinker if he or she would like the drink hot, and then alter with Tabasco sauce. This drink is just a Bloody Mary with tequila instead of vodka.

Fred Fud Pucker
1 1/2 oz. tequila
orange juice (fill almost to top)
1 oz. Galliano (float on top)
This drink is just the tequila version of the Harvey Wallbanger.

Iced Tea
1 oz. gin
1 oz. vodka
1 oz. rum
1 oz. tequila
splash sour mix
splash Rose's lime juice
cola to fill (after stirring)
Iced teas are very popular these days. If made correctly, they taste like real iced tea—but *feel* different. Another recipe appears on page 66 (shaken).

The following five drinks have been grouped together so you can learn them easily. They are all variations on each other.

Sloe Driver
1 1/2 oz. sloe gin
orange juice to fill
This is similar to a screwdriver, but contains sloe gin instead of vodka.

Comfortable Screw
1½ oz. Southern Comfort
orange juice to fill

This is similar to a screwdriver, but contains Southern Comfort instead of vodka. The word *comfort* or *comfortable* in the name of a drink means the recipe calls for some Southern Comfort.

Sloe Screw
Add 1 oz. sloe gin to a regular screwdriver.

Sloe Comfortable Screw
Add 1½ oz. Southern Comfort to a Sloe Screw. "Sloe + comfortable + screw" means: sloe gin + Southern Comfort + screwdriver (vodka and OJ).

Sloe Comfortable Screw Up Against the Wall
Float 1 oz. Galliano on top of a Sloe Comfortable Screw. (Most people blush when they order this drink.)

C. Fun Highballs

You don't really have to memorize these drinks because they aren't ordered too often. (Keep this book with you at the bar just in case.) They are listed alphabetically for easy reference. Make them as you would any other highball (see page 21 for steps).

Amaretto, Orange Juice, and Soda
1½ oz. amaretto
equal parts orange juice and soda to fill

Garnish with an orange slice.

Dark and Stormy
1½ oz. dark rum
ginger beer to fill

This delicious drink is popular in Bermuda, where they use Gosling's rum. If you can't find Gosling's, use another dark rum.

Gimlet Rickey
1½ oz. gin
1½ oz. Rose's lime juice
soda water to fill
Some people call this a "lime rickey."

Harvard Special
1 oz. Galliano
1½ oz. Pimm's No.1
ginger ale to fill
Garnish with orange slice.

Kahlúa and Iced Coffee
1½ oz. Kahlúa
iced coffee to fill

Kahlúa Root Beer Float
1 oz. Kahlúa
1 oz. cola
dash Galliano
club soda to fill
top with a scoop of vanilla ice cream
Do not serve on ice.

Kahlúa, Rum, and Soda
1½ oz. Kahlúa
1 oz. rum
soda water to fill

Mexicana
1½ oz. tequila
dash Rose's lime juice
dash grenadine
pineapple juice to fill

Orgasm
    1½ oz. vodka
    1½ oz. triple sec
    splash Rose's lime juice
    soda water, 7-up or Sprite to fill
This drink is similar to a Kamikaze, a shot drink. Tell your
friends that an Orgasm is just a big Kamikaze, or that a
Kamikaze is just a little Orgasm, and watch their eyes pop out.

Receptacle
    1½ oz. vodka
    splash each: orange, pineapple, cranberry juices
    top with 7-up or Sprite (after stirring)
Garnish with a cherry and an orange slice.

Shirley Temple
    dash grenadine
    7-up or Sprite to fill
Garnish with a cherry. Although few people actually order
Shirley Temples, you should memorize it, just in case. It's
something of a classic.

Very Screwy Driver
    1 oz. vodka
    1 oz. gin
    1 oz. tequila
    orange juice to fill
Garnish with a cherry and an orange slice.

Yellowbird
    1½ oz. rum
    ½ oz. triple sec
    orange juice to fill
Garnish with a cherry and an orange slice.

: II. STIRRED COCKTAILS :

A stirred cocktail contains about 3 ounces of liquid and is served in a cocktail glass (for a straight-up drink), in a rocks glass (for an on-the-rocks drink), or in one of the specialty glasses, if available (serve an Old Fashioned in an Old Fashioned glass, for example). Ask the drinker if he or she prefers a "rocks" or "up" drink, and then:

1. Fill shaker glass two-thirds full with ice.
2. Put smallest ingredient in first.
3. Eyeball the other ingredients—judge by sight how much to put in.
4. Stir *well*.
5. Strain the drink into serving glass.
6 Garnish, if necessary.

For more complete instructions, turn back to chapter 2, page 24.

A. Basic Stirred Drinks

Memorize these classics. Unless you work at a fancy bar, you probably won't make very many of these, but when you do they must be *perfect*. Martini drinkers are the fussiest people in the world. Be prepared.

MARTINIS

Martini
  1 part dry vermouth
  6–8 parts gin
Pour just a small splash of vermouth in the shaker and then a six-count of gin. (Melted ice brings the liquid content up to 3 ounces.) Garnish with an olive.

Dry Martini
1 part dry vermouth
10–12 parts gin

Pour a quick dash of vermouth into the shaker, and then add a six-count of gin. With such a high gin/vermouth ratio, it is impossible to eyeball proportions as recommended for other stirred cocktails. Garnish with an olive.

Extra Extra Dry Martini
6 parts gin
whisper "vermouth" softly over the gin

Garnish with an olive. By now, you've probably noticed that the way to dry out a martini is to reduce the amount of vermouth in the drink. Although you do not have to follow those exact steps for the extra extra dry martini, many people will order such a drink. They are too embarrassed to ask for "a glass of cold gin."

Fifty-Fifty
1 part gin
1 part dry vermouth

Pour in about a 3½-count of vermouth and then eyeball as much gin. Or, for advanced bartenders, pour both at the same time, for a 3½-count. Garnish with an olive.

Gibson
1 part dry vermouth
6–8 parts gin

Garnish with a cocktail onion. A Gibson is just a martini with a cocktail onion garnish instead of an olive.

Vodka Martini
1 part dry vermouth
6–8 parts vodka

Garnish with an olive. This is just a martini with vodka instead of gin. Reduce the vermouth for a dry drink.

Tequini (Tequila Martini)
  1 part dry vermouth
  6–8 parts tequila
Garnish with an olive and a lemon twist.

MANHATTANS

Manhattan
  1 part *sweet* vermouth
  4 parts blended whiskey or bourbon
  dash of bitters (optional—ask the drinker)
Garnish with a cherry. Notice that a Manhattan requires
sweet vermouth, whereas a martini contains dry vermouth.

Dry Manhattan
  1 part *dry* vermouth
  4 parts blended whiskey or bourbon
  dash bitters (optional)
Garnish with a cherry. For the dry martini, reduce the
amount of vermouth in the drink, but in a dry Manhattan,
change the *kind* of vermouth from sweet to dry.

Perfect Manhattan
  ½ part sweet vermouth
  ½ part dry vermouth
  4 parts blended whiskey or bourbon
  dash bitters (optional)
Garnish with a cherry.

Here are some Manhattan variations:

Rum Manhattan/Tequila Manhattan
Substitute the appropriate liquor for whiskey in a Manhattan.
In the tequila version, you may want to add a squeeze of lime
juice.

Rob Roy
Substitute Scotch for bourbon or blended whiskey in a regular Manhattan.

Comfort Manhattan
Substitute Southern Comfort for whiskey in a regular Manhattan.

GIMLETS

Gimlet
  1 part Rose's lime juice
  5 parts gin

Vodka Gimlet
Substitute vodka for gin in a regular gimlet.

OLD FASHIONEDS AND JULEPS

Prepare Old Fashioneds differently from other stirred cocktails:

1. Put a lump (or ½ teaspoon) sugar in the bottom of an Old Fashioned glass (or other lowball glass). That little bump on the bottom of the glass should remind you to do this step.
2. Add a dash or two of bitters to the sugar.
3. Put a handful of ice cubes in the glass.
4. Pour in 2½ ounces bourbon (about a six-count).
5. Add a splash of water or soda water.
6. Garnish with a cherry, an orange slice, and a lemon twist.

Tequila Old Fashioned/Rum Old Fashioned
Substitute appropriate liquor for bourbon in regular Old Fashioned.

Mint Julep
Make this drink exactly like the Old Fashioned, except:

1. Do not include bitters.
2. Garnish with mint sprigs, too.

This drink is more popular in the South than in the North. It is the traditional drink of celebration for the Kentucky Derby.

Brandy Julep
Substitute five-star brandy for bourbon in a mint julep.

STINGERS

Stinger
  1 part five-star brandy
  1 part white crème de menthe

A "sweet" stinger contains more crème de menthe. To memorize stinger ingredients, think of the *stinging*, cool mint flavor. If you remember that, the brandy bottle usually stands next to the crème de menthe on the back bar, so you can pick up both of them at the same time.

*Vodka Stinger/Scotch Stinger/Amaretto Stinger/Galliano
    Stinger*
Substitute the appropriate liquor or liqueur for brandy in a regular stinger.

International Stinger
  1 part Galliano
  1 part Metaxa
  2 parts white crème de menthe

Here are some drinks that are similar to stingers:

Mocha Mint
   1 part Kahlúa or coffee brandy
   1 part white crème de cacao
   1 part white crème de menthe

Peppermint Pattie
   1 part dark crème de cacao
   1 part white crème de menthe
Peppermint patties are brown on the outside, so use brown crème de cacao.

Flying Tiger
   1 part Galliano
   1 part vodka
   1 part white crème de menthe
This is just a Galliano stinger with vodka.

B. Popular Stirred Cocktails

Although they aren't classics, you'll get many requests for these drinks in a professional bar, so you should memorize them. Now for the good news—drinkers usually prefer these on the rocks, so you can mix them right in the glass (a rocks glass) rather than wasting time transferring from a shaker glass. The recipes are arranged according to common ingredients and variations, to help you memorize.

Black Russian
   2 parts vodka
   1 part Kahlúa

Mudslide
   1 part Kahlúa
   1 part Bailey's Irish Cream
   1 part vodka

This is similar to a Black Russian, but with the addition of Bailey's Irish Cream. You might want to shake this drink because cream does not mix readily.

Brave Bull
   1 part tequila
   1 part Kahlúa

Iguana
   1 part tequila
   1 part Kahlúa
   1 part vodka
An Iguana is similar to a Brave Bull, but with the addition of vodka.

Kahlúa and Amaretto
   1 part Kahlúa
   1 part amaretto

Black Watch
   1 part Kahlúa
   1 part Scotch
   splash of soda
Garnish with a lemon twist.

The Godfather
   3 parts whiskey
   1 part amaretto

The Godmother
Substitute vodka for whiskey in a Godfather.

Rusty Nail
   1 part Scotch
   1 part Drambuie

B and B
   1 part brandy
   1 part Benedictine

C. Fun Stirred Cocktails

You won't get many requests for these drinks, but they're here in case you need them. Recipes are arranged alphabetically in this section.

Blanche
   1 oz. anisette
   1 oz. triple sec
   1 oz. curaçao

Bombay Cocktail
   1 oz. brandy
   1 oz. curaçao
   ½ oz. dry vermouth
   ½ oz. sweet vermouth

Cool Whisper
   2 oz. Scotch
   ½ oz. dry vermouth
   ½ oz. sweet vermouth
Garnish with a lemon twist.

Dubonnet Cocktail
 1½ oz. Dubonnet
 1½ oz. gin
Garnish with a lemon twist.

Flying Grasshopper
 1 oz. green crème de menthe
 1 oz. white crème de cacao
 1 oz. vodka
This is similar to the Grasshopper, a shaken drink, but has vodka instead of the Grasshopper's cream.

French Breeze
 2 oz. Pernod
 1 oz. peppermint schnapps

Golden Glow
 1 oz. Galliano
 1 oz. Drambuie
 1 oz. gin
The word "golden" is your tip that the drink contains Galliano.

Jelly Bean
 1½ oz. five-star brandy
 ½ oz. anisette

Kahlúa and Brandy
 1½ oz. Kahlúa
 1½ oz. brandy

Latin Manhattan
 1 oz. rum
 1 oz. dry vermouth
 1 oz. sweet vermouth
 2 dashes bitters (optional)
Garnish with a lemon twist.

Negroni
    1 oz. gin
    1 oz. Campari
    1 oz. vermouth (either sweet or dry)

Saint Pat
    1 oz. green crème de menthe
    1 oz. Chartreuse (green)
    1 oz. Irish whiskey

Sazerac
    2 oz. bourbon
    1 tsp. sugar
    dash bitters
    dash Pernod
Garnish with a lemon twist.

Spanish Moss
    1 oz. Kahlúa
    1 oz. tequila
    1 oz. green crème de menthe

Wandering Minstrel
    1 oz. vodka
    ½ oz. Kahlúa
    ¾ oz. five-star brandy
    ¾ oz. white crème de menthe

Yale
    1½ oz. gin
    ½ oz. dry vermouth
    dash Crème Yvette (blue)
    dash bitters (optional)

:III. SHAKEN DRINKS:

To refresh your memory, here's a quick reminder how to make shaken drinks. For more details, review pages 24-28 in chapter 2.

1. Fill the shaker glass two-thirds full with ice.
2. Pour in the liquor first.
3. Add juices and other ingredients.
4. Put the shaker shell over the glass and give the top a little tap to seal it in place.
5. Holding the top and bottom of the shaker, shake up and down.
6. Hit the shell at the frost line with the heel of your hand to break the seal.
7. Turn the whole shaker over (holding the two pieces together).
8. Remove the glass from inside the shell.
9. Put the strainer over the shell and strain the drink into the serving glass.
10. Garnish, if necessary.

Follow this procedure for all the basic shaken drinks and for all other shaken drinks served straight up. Later, you'll read about a shortcut suitable for some drinks.

The recipes in the first two sections are arranged in groups of similar recipes, in order to make them easier to master. You may find these recipes easy to remember, and then forge ahead into the real world only to encounter a new problem— you've memorized ingredients and proportions, but forgotten whether to shake or stir! As a general rule, *you should shake fruit juice, sour mix, sugar, egg and cream drinks, or cocktails that contain other difficult-to-mix ingredients*. Some of the multiliqueur drinks in the stirred section might actually mix better when shaken, if you prefer.

Many of these recipes call for juice from half a lemon and 1 teaspoon sugar. When both of these ingredients appear together in the recipe, you can substitute sour mix. Keep sour mix already prepared, bottled, and with a speedpourer in it, on your bar. Juice from half a lemon and 1 teaspoon sugar equals about a three-count from the speedpourer (adjust according to your preferences). Likewise, if the recipe calls for 1 to 1½ ounces of sour mix, you can substitute juice from half a lemon and 1 teaspoon sugar.

A. Basic Shaken Cocktails

SOURS

Whiskey Sour
  2 oz. bourbon or blended whiskey
  juice of ½ lemon
  1 tsp. sugar
Garnish with a cherry and an orange slice.

The following drink, a Ward Eight, is similar to the whiskey sour; it is merely a whiskey sour plus grenadine.

Ward Eight
  2 oz. bourbon or blended whiskey
  juice of ½ lemon
  1 tsp. sugar
  ½ oz. grenadine
Garnish with a cherry and an orange slice.

Other whiskey sour variations:

Rum Sour/Vodka Sour/Gin Sour/Tequila Sour
Substitute appropriate liquor for whiskey in a regular whiskey sour.

Apricot Sour
Substitute apricot brandy for whiskey in a regular whiskey sour.

Scotch Sour
   2 oz. Scotch
   juice of ½ lime
   1 tsp. sugar
Garnish with a cherry and an orange slice. This recipe calls for *lime* juice instead of lemon, so you cannot use sour mix in this drink.

Comfort Sour
Substitute Southern Comfort for whiskey in a whiskey sour.

DAIQUIRI VARIATIONS

Daiquiri
   2 oz. rum
   juice of ½ lime
   1 tsp. sugar
A daiquiri contains lime juice, not lemon, so you cannot use sour mix in it. Some bars stock a premixed lime and sugar mixture (such as Quik-Lime), but it is not very common. In a crowded, busy bar, some bartenders make daiquiris with sour mix (like a rum sour) and then squeeze a couple of lime wedges on the top to fool the customer's taste buds. Good idea!

The next drink, the Bacardi Cocktail, is similar to the daiquiri, but with the addition of grenadine.

Bacardi Cocktail
   2 oz. Bacardi rum
   juice of ½ lime
   1 tsp. sugar
   ½ oz. grenadine

The next drink, the Mai Tai, is based on the Bacardi Cocktail, but with several extra ingredients.

Mai Tai
    2 oz. rum
    juice from ½ lime
    1 tsp. sugar
    ½ oz. grenadine
    ½ oz. orgeat (almond syrup)
    1 oz. curaçao
Garnish with a cherry and a pineapple slice.

MARGARITAS

Margarita
    2 oz. tequila
    ½ oz. triple sec
    juice of ½ lime
    strain into a salt-rimmed glass (cocktail or champagne glass)
For instructions on how to rim the glass with salt, refer to the Salty Dog recipe on page 34. This is the shaken version of this drink. For a blended Margarita, see page 77.

As an interesting variation on the shaken drink, some bars make "upside-down Margaritas." A customer lays his or her head down on the bar and the bartender pours the Margarita ingredients—one by one—into the customer's open mouth (topping it all off with a pinch of salt, of course). Then the customer jumps up and down to shake the drink. No glasses to wash!

COLLINSES

Tom Collins
    2 oz. gin
    juice of ½ lemon
    1 tsp. sugar

Shake, strain into Collins glass, and top with soda water. Garnish with a cherry and an orange slice.

The main difference between a sour and a Collins is the addition of soda water which carbonates the Collins. Also, the whiskey sour is usually served without ice in a sour glass, whereas the Collins goes over ice into a highball-like, frosted Collins glass.

The following drinks—the Singapore Sling, sloe gin fizz, vodka Collins, John Collins, rum Collins, and tequila Collins—are all similar to the Tom Collins. If you learn just their changes, it will be easier to remember how to make these drinks.

Singapore Sling
2 oz. gin
1/2 oz. wild cherry brandy
juice of 1/2 lemon
1 tsp. sugar

Shake, strain into Collins glass, and top with soda water. Garnish with a cherry and an orange slice. This drink is a Tom Collins plus wild cherry brandy.

Sloe Gin Fizz
2 oz. sloe gin
juice of 1/2 lemon
1 tsp. sugar

Shake, strain into Collins glass, and top with soda water. Garnish with a cherry and an orange slice. This is a Tom Collins with sloe gin substituted for gin.

John Collins
Substitute whiskey for gin in a Tom Collins.

Vodka Collins/Rum Collins/Tequila Collins
Substitute the appropriate liquor for gin in a Tom Collins.

That's it for the basic shaken drinks. If you think about it, you only have to memorize four drinks, and the rest are variations:

1. Whiskey Sour
   a. Ward Eight (add grenadine)
   b. Scotch Sour (substitute Scotch for bourbon and lime juice for lemon juice)
   c. Rum Sour ⎫
   d. Gin Sour ⎪ (substitute appropriate
   e. Vodka Sour ⎬ liquor for whiskey)
   f. Tequila Sour ⎪
   g. Apricot Sour ⎭
   h. Comfort Sour (substitute Southern Comfort for whiskey)
2. Daiquiri
   a. Bacardi (add grenadine)
   b. Mai Tai (add grenadine, orgeat, curaçao, and garnishes)
3. Margarita
4. Tom Collins
   a. Singapore Sling (add wild cherry brandy)
   b. Sloe Gin Fizz (substitute sloe gin for gin)
   c. John Collins (substitute whiskey for gin)
   d. Vodka Collins ⎫
   e. Rum Collins ⎬ (substitute appropriate liquor for whiskey)
   f. Tequila Collins ⎭

B. Popular Shaken Drinks

Some of these drinks have become so popular in recent years that they're practically basics, so you should definitely memorize them if you plan to work in a bar some day. If you tend bar in a busy place, though, going through the whole shaker routine gets bothersome after a while. (How often do you see a speed-oriented bartender wasting time by carefully shaking a mere White Russian on the rocks? Rarely.)

Instead, use a half-shell (also called a short shaker) for shaken drinks on the rocks. This gadget is a small, usually plastic shaker *shell* that fits over regular rocks and highball glasses. If you're using disposable plastic glasses, mix the drink in a highball glass and use a lowball glass for the half-shell.

Short-shaking:

1. Pour the drink ingredients over ice in the appropriate glass.
2. Fit the short shaker securely over the glass.
3. Shake up and down a few times.
4. Remove the shaker.

Quick and simple! This method is not as thorough and neat as the regular shaker technique, and *cannot* be used for straight-up cocktails, but it saves valuable time in some instances when you're in a hurry.

These drinks are arranged according to similar ingredients, to help you memorize.

Sombrero
    1½ oz. coffee brandy
    milk or cream to fill
Serve over ice in a rocks glass. Some bartenders prefer *not* to shake their sombreros, the idea being that the cream floats on top like a hat.

Kahlúa Sombrero
Substitute Kahlúa for coffee brandy in a sombrero.

Italian Sombrero
Substitute amaretto for coffee brandy in a sombrero.

Amaretto and Cream
   1½ oz. amaretto
   1½ oz. cream
Serve in a rocks or cocktail glass.

Toasted Almond
   1½ oz. Kahlúa or coffee brandy
   1½ oz. amaretto
   milk or cream to fill
Serve over ice in a rocks or highball glass.

Creamsicle
   1½ oz. amaretto
   1½ oz. orange juice
   milk or cream to fill
Usually served over ice in a rocks or highball glass. This drink
tastes like an ice cream Creamsicle.

White Russian
   2 oz. vodka
   1 oz. Kahlúa or coffee brandy
   ½ oz. cream

Serve in a rocks glass. This drink, without the cream, is a Black Russian (a stirred drink).

Dirty Bird
An unstirred, unshaken White Russian.

Grasshopper
 1 oz. green crème de menthe
 1 oz. white crème de cacao
 1 oz. cream
Serve in a rocks or cocktail glass (usually cocktail).

Mexican Grasshopper
Substitute Kahlúa for white crème de cacao in a Grasshopper.

Vodka Grasshopper
 3/4 oz. green crème de menthe
 3/4 oz. white crème de cacao
 3/4 oz. vodka
 3/4 oz. cream
Serve in a rocks or cocktail glass.

Girl Scout Cookie
 1 oz. dark crème de cacao
 1 oz. white crème de menthe
 1 oz. cream
This is a Grasshopper with the liqueurs' colors reversed. Girl Scout mint cookies contain chocolate on the outside (like dark crème de cacao) and white mint cookie on the inside (white crème de menthe and cream).

Alexander
   1 oz. gin
   1 oz. dark crème de cacao
   1 oz. cream
Serve in a rocks or cocktail glass.

Brandy Alexander
Substitute five-star brandy for gin in an Alexander. Dust the top with nutmeg.

Pink Squirrel
   1 oz. crème de noyaux
   1 oz. white crème de cacao
   1 oz. cream
Usually served straight up in a cocktail glass. Memorize these ingredients by remembering "pink"—crème de noyaux is red; mixed with cream it becomes pink. Squirrels eat nuts; crème de noyaux is almond-flavored.

Banshee
   1 oz. crème de banana
   1 oz. white crème de cacao
   1 oz. cream
Usually served straight up in a cocktail glass. This drink is similar to a Pink Squirrel, but with crème de banana instead of crème de noyaux. The first part of the word *ban*shee is the same as the first part of the word *ban*ana.

Melonball
   2 oz. Midori
   1 oz. vodka
   orange or grapefruit juice to fill
Serve over ice in a highball glass.

Pearl Harbor
Substitute pineapple juice for orange or grapefruit juice in a Melonball.

Honolulu Hammer
  1½ oz. vodka
  ½ oz. amaretto
  dash grenadine
  splash pineapple juice
Usually served straight up in a cocktail or shot glass.

Alabama Slammer
  1 oz. Southern Comfort
  1 oz. vodka
  dash grenadine
  dash sour mix
  splash orange juice
Usually served straight up in a cocktail or shot glass.

Cherry Bomb
Substitute cherry brandy for apricot in an Apricot Bomb.

Apricot Bomb
  1½ oz. apricot brandy
  2 oz. vodka
  1½ oz. triple sec
  2 oz. sour mix
Serve over ice in a highball glass.

Scarlett O'Hara
  1½ oz. Southern Comfort
  1½ oz. cranberry juice
  juice of ½ lime
Think of *Scarlett* and remember that *scarlet* cranberry juice gives the drink its red color. Scarlett O'Hara of *Gone with the Wind* movie fame reminds most people of the South, so it should be easy to remember that Southern Comfort is the liquor in the drink.

Zombie

    2 oz. rum
    1 oz. Jamaican rum
    1/2 oz. apricot brandy
    1 oz. orange juice
    1 oz. pineapple juice

Shake and strain over fresh ice into a highball glass. Float on top 1/2 oz. 151-proof rum. Garnish with a pineapple slice or chunk and a cherry. Serve with straws.

Zombie (variation)

    1 oz. light rum
    1/2 oz. Jamaican rum
    1/2 oz. crème de noyaux
    1/2 oz. triple sec
    1 oz. lemon juice
    1 oz. orange juice

Shake, strain into highball glass with fresh ice, and top with soda water. Garnish with a pineapple slice or chunk and a cherry.

Iced Tea

    1 oz. vodka
    1 oz. gin
    1 oz. tequila
    1 oz. triple sec
    splash lemon juice

Shake, strain over fresh ice in a highball glass, and fill with cola. When made correctly, this tastes like real iced tea. See page 41 for a slightly different recipe.

Planter's Punch
  2 oz. rum
  1 oz. Myers's rum (Jamaican)
  juice of 1 lime
  1 tsp. sugar
Shake and fill with soda water. Garnish with an orange slice and a cherry.

Planter's Punch (variation)
  2 oz. rum
  juice of ½ lemon
  1 tsp. sugar
  splash orange juice
  splash pineapple juice
Shake, then swirl on top ½ oz. Myers's rum (Jamaican) and ½ oz. curaçao. Garnish with a cherry and an orange slice. Serve with straws. The liquors on top give the drink its "punch" when it is sipped through a straw. The drinker finishes the bottom part first and gets an extra boost from the rum and curaçao at the end.

Those Planter's Punch recipes look tough to memorize, don't they? You're in luck—the Myers's rum bottle has a recipe printed right on the label, so you can cheat if necessary.

EGGNOGS

Standard Eggnog
  1 egg
  1 tsp. sugar
  1½ oz. liquor (perhaps brandy, whiskey, rum, or a combination)
  6 oz. milk
Shake with ice and strain into highball glass without ice. Dust with nutmeg.

Fruity Eggnog
   1 egg
   ½ oz. triple sec
   2 oz. apricot brandy
   6 oz. milk
Shake with ice and strain into highball glass without ice. Dust
with nutmeg.

For an extra-foamy nog, try mixing these eggnogs in the
blender. For an eggnog punch recipe, see page 114.

C. Fun Shaken Drinks

Just glance through these drinks to see if they sound good—
don't worry about memorizing them. They are listed alphabetically for easy reference.

Between the Sheets
   1 oz. five-star brandy
   1 oz. triple sec
   1 oz. rum

Bullshot
   1½ oz. vodka
   4 oz. beef boullion
   dash Worcestershire sauce
Shake without ice, strain into highball glass with ice, and garnish
with a lemon twist. This drink is a popular morning-after, "hair-
of-the-dog" remedy.

California Lemonade
   2 oz. blended whiskey
   1 oz. sour mix
   juice of 1 lime
   dash grenadine

Shake, strain into Collins glass over fresh ice, and fill with soda water. Garnish with an orange slice, lemon twist, and a cherry.

California Root Beer
  1½ oz. Kahlúa
  1½ oz. milk
  1 oz. Galliano
Shake in highball glass, and fill with cola.

Cherry Rum
  1½ oz. rum
  ½ oz. cherry brandy
  ½ oz. cream

Chocolate Daisy
  1½ oz. five-star brandy
  1½ oz. port wine
  juice of ½ lemon
  1 tsp. sugar
  splash grenadine

Chocolate Mint Rum
  1 oz. rum
  ½ oz. dark crème de cacao
  1 oz. white crème de menthe
  ½ oz. cream
Usually served on the rocks.

Chuckie
  1½ oz. vodka
  dash curaçao
  splash pineapple juice
  splash orange juice
Shake, strain into rocks glass with fresh ice, and top with soda. Garnish with a cherry.

Cream Puff
  2 oz. rum
  1 oz. cream
  1 tsp. sugar

Creamy Mocha Mint
  ¾ oz. Kahlúa or coffee brandy
  ¾ oz. white crème de cacao
  ¾ oz. white crème de menthe
  ¾ oz. cream

Cuban Special
  1 oz. rum
  dash triple sec
  splash pineapple juice
  juice of ½ lime
Garnish with a cherry.

Dirty Mother
  1½ oz. Kahlúa or coffee brandy
  1½ oz. tequila
  milk or cream to fill
Strain over fresh ice into a rocks or highball glass.

Dirty Virgin
  2 oz. gin
  1 oz. dark crème de cacao

El Presidente Herminio
  1½ oz. rum
  ½ oz. crème de banana
  ½ oz. curaçao
  splash orange juice
  splash pineapple juice
Strain over fresh ice into lowball glass.

Fan
   2 oz. Scotch
   1 oz. triple sec or Cointreau
   1 oz. grapefruit juice

French 75—see page 91.

Georgia Cream
   1 oz. peach brandy
   1 oz. white crème de cacao
   1 oz. cream

Golden Apple
   1 oz. Galliano
   ½ oz. applejack
   ½ oz. white crème de cacao
Strain into a champagne glass rimmed with maraschino cherry
juice and dipped in coconut powder.

Golden Cadillac
   1 oz. Galliano
   1 oz. white crème de cacao
   1 oz. cream

Golden Dream
   1 oz. Galliano
   ½ oz. triple sec or Cointreau
   ½ oz. cream
   1½ oz. orange juice

Guana Grabber
   1 oz. light rum
   1 oz. dark rum
   1 oz. coconut rum (such as Malibu or Cocoribe)
   3 oz. pineapple juice
   1 oz. grapefruit juice
   dash grenadine

Harvard
1½ oz. five-star brandy
½ oz. dry vermouth
1 tsp. grenadine
juice of ½ lemon

Jack Rose
2 oz. applejack
juice of ½ lemon
1 tsp. grenadine

Jamaican Cream
1 oz. Jamaican rum
1 oz. triple sec
1 oz. cream

James Bond 007
A vodka martini—shaken, not stirred. (Although once he ordered bourbon, no ice.)

Kahlúa Cream Soda
1 oz. Kahlúa
4 oz. cream
Shake, strain into highball glass with ice, and fill with soda water.

Mocha Cream
1 oz. Kahlúa or coffee brandy
1 oz. white crème de cacao
1 oz. cream

Pink Lady
2 oz. gin
1 oz. cream
½ oz. grenadine
1 egg white
Strain into cocktail glass.

Ramos Fizz
    1½ oz. gin
    juice of ½ lemon
    juice of ½ lime
    1½ oz. cream
    ½ tsp. sugar
    1 egg white
Strain. This is a popular morning-after, "hair-of-the-dog"
remedy.

Red Russian
    1 oz. strawberry liqueur
    1 oz. vodka
    1 oz. cream

Russian Bear
    1 oz. vodka
    1 oz. dark crème de cacao
    1 oz. cream

Sidecar
    1 oz. five-star brandy
    1 oz. triple sec
    juice of ½ lemon
Strain into cocktail glass.

Tam-O'-Shanter (Irish Sombrero)
    1 oz. Kahlúa or coffee brandy
    ½ oz. Irish Whiskey
    milk to fill
Shake with ice in highball glass.

Tootsie Roll
    1½ oz. Kahlúa
    1½ oz. dark crème de cacao
    orange juice to fill
Shake with ice in highball glass. When made correctly, this
drink tastes like a Tootsie Roll.

Tropical Gold
  1 oz. rum or vodka
  ½ oz. crème de banana
  orange juice to fill
Shake in highball glass with ice. Garnish with an orange slice
and pineapple chunk.

Velvet Kiss
  1 oz. gin
  ½ oz. crème de banana
  1 oz. cream
  splash pineapple juice
  splash grenadine

: IV. BLENDED DRINKS :

Blended drinks (also called freezes or frozen drinks) taste incredibly delicious. Even the most stubborn and steadfast beer or
whiskey drinkers have trouble refusing a frosty piña colada on a
hot day!
  To make blender drinks, follow a few simple steps:

1. Use only a heavy-duty blender.
2. With the machine off, mix the ingredients in the blender.
    Put the liquor in first, followed by mixers, then fruit, and
    finally ice (enough ice so the blender is three-quarters
    full).

3. Keeping fingers, hair, loose clothing, and small children away from blender, put the lid on.
4. While holding the lid down with one hand, start the machine on low speed. After the initial mixing, change up to high speed until the ingredients are well blended.

Recipes are divided into six categories to help you memorize the ones you like: Coladas, Daiquiris, Margaritas, Tropical Drinks, Ice Cream Drinks, and Make Your Own.

COLADAS

Piña Colada
   4–6 oz. rum
   5–7 oz. coconut cream (comes in a can at the supermarket or liquor store.)
   10 oz. pineapple juice
Blend with ice. Garnish with cherry and pineapple chunk.

If you don't want to measure or use the amounts given in this formula (in other words, if you just want to throw the ingredients in the blender any old way), follow this basic formula:

2 parts pineapple juice
1 part coconut cream
as much rum as you want (about 1 part)

Hints:

● If you don't want a sweet piña colada, reduce the amount of coconut cream.
● For a slushy drink, add more ice.
● For a special touch, add a splash of grenadine and you'll have pink piñas.
● For a richer rum flavor, use golden or dark rum as well as light rum.

Midori Colada
  2 parts Midori (2 oz.)
  1 part rum (1 oz.)
  4 parts pineapple juice (4 oz.)
  2 parts coconut cream (2 oz.)
Blend with ice. Garnish with a cherry, pineapple chunk, and/
or melonball. For hints on how to alter or improve your
Midori colada, see the notes under the piña colada recipe.

DAIQUIRIS

Frozen Daiquiri
  2 oz. rum
  1/2 oz. triple sec
  1 1/2 oz. lime juice
  1 tsp. sugar
Blend with ice.

Banana Daiquiri
  2 oz. rum
  1/2 oz. crème de cacao (either color)
  1/2 oz. crème de banana (optional)
  1 sliced banana
Blend with ice.

Strawberry Daiquiri
　2 oz. rum
　½ oz. strawberry liqueur (optional)
　½ cup fresh or frozen strawberries
　1 tsp. sugar
Blend with ice.

Peach Daiquiri
Add to frozen daiquiri: 1 canned peach half with 1 oz. juice or
½ sliced, fresh peach (more if desired). Optional: add ½ oz.
peach flavored brandy.

　You can keep adjusting the frozen daiquiri recipe for every
fruit in the world. If you have a favorite fruit or flavoring,
throw it into the blender with some rum, sour mix, and ice.

MARGARITAS

Margarita
　2 oz. tequila
　1 oz. triple sec
　4 oz. lemon or lime juice
　2 tsp. sugar
Blend with or without ice. Garnish with lime slice (optional),
and serve in cocktail or champagne glass rimmed with salt.
　For instructions on how to rim glass with salt, refer to the
Salty Dog recipe on page 34.

Strawberry Margarita
　2 oz. tequila
　1 oz. triple sec
　4 oz. lemon or lime juice
　½ cup strawberries, fresh or frozen
　1 oz. strawberry liqueur or 2 tsp. sugar
Blend with ice. Garnish with a fresh strawberry or a lime
slice.

Midori Margarita
　　2 oz. tequila
　　1½ oz. Midori
　　1½ oz. sour mix
Blend with ice. Serve in salted cocktail or champagne glass (salt optional).

TROPICAL DRINKS

Tropical Storm
　　2 oz. rum (light, dark, or both)
　　1 oz. crème de banana
　　½ medium banana
　　4 oz. orange juice
　　dash grenadine
Blend with ice. Garnish with a cherry and an orange slice.

Scorpion
　　3 oz. light rum
　　½ oz. brandy
　　2 oz. lemon juice
　　3 oz. orange juice
Blend with ice. Garnish with a cherry
and an orange slice.

Blue Hawaiian
　　2 oz. rum
　　1 oz. blue curaçao
　　1 oz. sour mix
　　1 oz. orange juice
　　1 oz. pineapple juice
Blend with ice.

Jump-Up-and-Kiss-Me
    2 oz. Galliano
    2 oz. rum
    ½ oz. apricot brandy
    juice of 1 lemon
    1 oz. pineapple juice
    2 egg whites
Blend with ice. Serve in brandy snifter.

ICE CREAM DRINKS

Mississippi Mud
    1½ oz. Southern Comfort
    1½ oz. Kahlúa or coffee brandy
    2 scoops vanilla ice cream
Blend *without* ice. Garnish with chocolate shavings.

Hammer
    1 oz. Kahlúa or coffee brandy
    1 oz. light rum
    2 scoops vanilla ice cream
Blend *without* ice.

Blended White Russian
    1 oz. Kahlúa
    2 oz. vodka
    2 scoops vanilla ice cream
Blend *without* ice.

Coffee/Cocoa Brandy Alexander
    1 oz. Kahlúa, coffee brandy, *or* crème de cacao
    1 oz. brandy or cognac
    2 scoops vanilla ice cream
Blend *without* ice.

Coffee Cacao Cream
  ½ cup crème de cacao
  splash white crème de menthe
  ½ cup cold black coffee
  1 scoop vanilla ice cream
Blend with ice.

MAKE YOUR OWN

Bored with the ordinary ice cream recipes listed here? Just convert your favorite shaken cream or milk drink into a blended ice-cream drink. For example, the Toasted Almond recipe on page 62 becomes:

Toasted Almond (Ice Cream Version)
  1½ oz. Kahlúa or coffee brandy
  1 oz. Amaretto
  2 scoops vanilla ice cream
Blend without ice.

Or, the Grasshopper recipe on page 63 becomes:

Grasshopper (Ice Cream Version)
  1–1½ oz. green crème de menthe
  1–1½ oz. white crème de cacao
  2 scoops vanilla ice cream
Blend without ice.

Use your imagination. Blend Kahlúa with coffee ice cream or crème de menthe with chocolate. The possibilities are endless . . . if fattening!

: V. HOT DRINKS :

COFFEE DRINKS

Amaretto Café
  1½ oz. amaretto
  hot black coffee
Stir. Top with whipped cream

Café Mexicano
  1 oz. Kahlúa
  ½ oz. tequila
  hot black coffee
Stir. Garnish as desired.

Creamy Irish Coffee
  1½ oz. Bailey's Irish Cream
  hot black coffee
Stir. Top with whipped cream.

Irish Coffee
  1½ oz. Irish whiskey
  1 tsp. sugar
  hot black coffee
Stir. Top with whipped cream.

Jamaican Coffee
  1 oz. Tia Maria (or Kahlúa)
  ¾ oz. rum
  hot black coffee
Stir. Top with whipped cream, if desired, and dust with
nutmeg.

Kahlúa Irish Coffee
  1 oz. Kahlúa
  1 oz. Irish whiskey *or* 1 oz. Bailey's Irish Cream
  hot black coffee
Stir. Garnish as desired.

Kioki Coffee
  1 oz. Kahlúa
  ½ oz. brandy
  hot black coffee
Stir. Garnish as desired.

Mexican Coffee
  1½ oz. Kahlúa
  hot black coffee
Stir. Top with whipped cream, if desired, and dust with nutmeg or add cinnamon stick.

Nutty Coffee
  1 oz. amaretto
  ½ oz. Frangelico
  hot black coffee
Stir. Top with whipped cream.

Roman Coffee
  1½ oz. Galliano
  hot black coffee
Stir. Top with whipped cream.

Other Hot Drinks

Chimney Fire
  1½ oz. amaretto
  hot cider
Garnish with cinnamon stick.

Chimney Fire Variations
Substitute Southern Comfort or dark rum for amaretto.

Comfort Mocha
  1½ oz. Southern Comfort
  1 tsp. instant cocoa or hot chocolate
  1 tsp. instant coffee
Add boiling water. Top with whipped cream if desired.

Good Night
  2 oz. rum
  1 tsp. sugar
  warm milk
Serve in mug. Dust with nutmeg.

Grog
  1½ oz. rum
  1 tsp. sugar
  juice of ¼ lemon
  boiling water

Hot Buttered Rum
  2 oz. rum
  1 tsp. sugar
  1 tsp. butter
  boiling water
Dust with nutmeg.

Hot Italian
  2 oz. amaretto
  warm orange juice
Garnish with cinnamon stick.

Hot Toddy
  2 oz. whiskey
  1 tsp. sugar
  boiling water
Serve in mug. Garnish with lemon slice and dust with nutmeg or add cinnamon stick.

Hot Wine Lemonade
  1½ oz. red wine
  juice of ½–1 lemon
  1½ tsp. sugar
  boiling water
Garnish with lemon twist.

Italian Tea
  1½ oz. amaretto
  1 tsp. sugar (optional)
  hot tea
Stir. Top with whipped cream.

Kahlúa and Hot Chocolate
  1 oz. Kahlúa
  hot chocolate
Top with whipped cream.

Tom & Jerry
Beat until stiff:
  1 egg white
  2 tsp. sugar
  pinch baking soda
  ½ oz. rum
Take *1 tbsp*. of this batter and mix it with:
  2 tbsp. hot milk
  1½ oz. rum
Put in warm mug, fill mug with more hot milk. Float on top ½ oz. five-star brandy. Dust with nutmeg.

: VI. FLAME DRINKS :

To flame a drink safely, first warm only one teaspoon of the required liquor over a match flame, then ignite. Once it is lit, *carefully* pour it over the prepared recipe. Stand back!

This method is safer than lighting the liquor right in the glass.

Blue Blazer
  2½ oz. whiskey
  2½ oz. boiling water
Pour these liquids into two separate mugs. Ignite the whiskey. *Mix* by pouring back and forth several times between the two mugs. Garnish with a lemon twist and serve in a warm on-the-rocks glass.

In a darkened room, the mixing process will appear as though you are pouring liquid, blue fire.

As an option, you may add 1 tbsp. honey to the above ingredients.

Southern Blazer
Substitute 1½ oz. Southern Comfort and 1 oz. Kahlúa for the whiskey in the Blue Blazer recipe. After mixing, add two dashes of bitters and garnish with an orange slice.

Brandy Blazer
> 2 oz. five-star brandy
> 1 tsp. sugar
> 1 piece orange peel
> 1 lemon twist

Put ingredients in Old Fashioned or rocks glass. Ignite. Stir with bar spoon, then strain into thick, stemmed glass.

Café Royale
> One cube of sugar soaked in five-star brandy

Ignite in spoon over mug of hot black coffee. Drop in coffee as sugar carmelizes and flame dies out.

Flaming Harbor Light
In a shot glass, layer:
> 1 part Kahlúa
> 1 part tequila
> 1 part 151-proof rum

Ignite.

Lighthouse
> 1 part Galliano
> 1 part dry vermouth

Ignite Galliano in shot glass and pour it over dry vermouth in a pony glass. May be served on the rocks in a champagne glass and garnished with a lemon slice.

: VII. POUSSE-CAFÉS :

Pousse-cafés are layered drinks. When you pour several liquids carefully into a pony glass, the heaviest ones stay on the bottom and the lightest ones float to the top, thus creating layers.

To make a pousse-café, be careful! Move slowly. Pour each liquid onto the bar spoon handle (that's why the bar spoon handle is twisted) and let it slide gently into the pony glass via the edge of the glass. Always pour the heaviest liquid first, then the next heaviest, and so on.

The recipes here list the ingredients from heaviest to lightest, so pour them in the order given.

Angel's Delight
   1 part grenadine
   1 part triple sec
   1 part Crème Yvette
   1 part cream

Angel's Kiss
   1 part white crème de cacao
   1 part Crème Yvette
   1 part five-star brandy
   1 part cream

Angel's Tip
   1 part brown crème de cacao
   1 part cream
Stick a toothpick through a cherry and balance it on top of the glass.

Angel's Wing
   1 part white crème de cacao
   1 part five-star brandy
   1 part cream

Christmas
   1 part grenadine
   2 parts green crème de menthe

Fifth Avenue
   1 part dark crème de cacao
   1 part apricot brandy
   1 part cream

King Alphonse
An angel's tip without the cherry.

King's Cup
   2 parts Galliano
   1 part cream .

Princess
   3 parts apricot brandy
   1 part cream

Stars and Stripes
   1 part grenadine
   1 part heavy cream
   1 part Crème Yvette

Make Your Own Pousse-Café

Each liqueur has a specific weight. The key to making pousse-cafés is to put the heaviest liqueur in the glass first, then the next heaviest, and so on. Cream floats on the top. Technically, you could probably layer all of the liqueurs listed here on top of each other, but most pousse-cafés have only three to five layers.

The following chart assigns numbers to the relative weights of the most popular pousse-café liqueurs, from heaviest to lightest:

Liqueur	*Relative Weight*
Anisette (50 proof)	17.8
Crème de noyaux (50 proof)	17.7
Crème de menthe (60 proof)	15.9
Crème de banana (50 proof)	15.0
Maraschino liqueur (50 proof)	14.9
Coffee liqueur (50 proof)	14.2
Cherry liqueur (48 proof)	12.7
Parfait Amour (50 proof)	12.7

Blue curaçao (60 proof)	11.7
Blackberry liqueur (50 proof)	11.2
Apricot liqueur (58 proof)	10.0
Orange curaçao (60 proof)	9.8
Triple sec (60 proof)	9.8
Coffee brandy (70 proof)	9.0
Peach brandy (70 proof)	7.0
Cherry brandy (70 proof)	6.8
Blackberry brandy (70 proof)	6.7
Apricot brandy (70 proof)	6.6
Rock and Rye liqueur (60 proof)	6.5
Ginger brandy (70 proof)	6.1
Peppermint schnapps (60 proof)	5.2
Kummel (78 proof)	4.2
Peach liqueur (60 proof)	4.1
Sloe gin (60 proof)	4.0

: VIII. WINE AND CHAMPAGNE DRINKS :

WINE DRINKS

Kir
dash creme de cassis
dry white wine, chilled, to fill
Serve in a wine glass.

Spritzer
1 part white wine
1 part club soda
Serve on ice with a lemon twist in a large wine glass or tall
frosted glass.

Vermouth Aperitif
Serve sweet vermouth on ice with a lemon twist.

Vermouth Half and Half
   1 part sweet vermouth
   1 part dry vermouth
Ice, stir, strain into wine glass. Fill with soda water. Garnish with a lemon twist.

For more wine drink recipes, see the Cooler section of this chapter.

CHAMPAGNE DRINKS

Bubbling Mint
   ½ oz. green crème de menthe
   champagne to fill
Serve in champagne glass.

Caribbean Champagne
   splash rum
   splash crème de banana
Pour into champagne glass. Add champagne to fill. Garnish with banana slice.

Champagne Cocktail
   glass of champagne
   2 dashes bitters
   1 tsp. sugar
Stir, without ice. Garnish with extra long spiral twist of lemon.

Champagne Cooler
This drink is listed in the Coolers section of this chapter, page 92.

Champagne Fizz
  2 oz. gin
  1 oz. sour mix
Shake, strain into highball glass with ice, and fill with champagne.

French 75
In shaker glass with ice, pour:
  1 oz. gin
  2 oz. sour mix
Shake, strain over ice into highball or Collins glass. Add champagne to fill. Garnish with an orange slice and a cherry.

Kir Royale
  dash crème de cassis
  chilled champagne to fill
Serve in a champagne glass.

Mimosa
  1 part champagne
  1 part orange juice
  dash triple sec
Garnish with an orange slice.

Midori Mimosa
  2 oz. Midori
  2 tsp. lime juice
  champagne to fill
Garnish with a lime wedge and strawberries (optional).

: IX. COOLERS :

Serve these drinks over ice in tall, frosty glasses.

At a busy bar, if a customer orders a wine cooler or spritzer, just pour about 3 ounces wine over ice in a tall glass and fill with soda water.

WINE AND CHAMPAGNE COOLERS

Champagne Cooler
  1 oz. brandy
  1 oz. Cointreau or triple sec
  champagne to fill
Garnish with mint sprigs.

Country Club Cooler
  3 oz. dry vermouth
  1 tsp. grenadine
  soda water to fill

Pineapple-Wine Cooler
  2½ oz. dry white wine
  2½ oz. pineapple juice
  soda water to fill
Garnish with a lemon and orange twist (extra long spirals). As an option, you may add 1 oz. rum before you pour in the soda water.

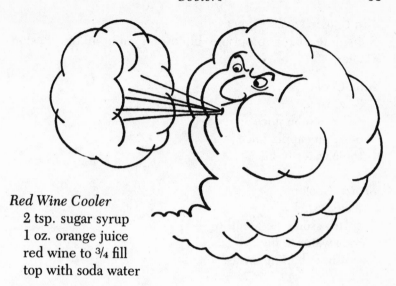

Red Wine Cooler
    2 tsp. sugar syrup
    1 oz. orange juice
    red wine to ¾ fill
    top with soda water

White Wine Cooler
    1 tsp. sugar syrup
    white wine to ¾ fill
    top with soda
Garnish with mint sprigs.

LIQUOR-BASED COOLERS

Apricot Cooler
    1½ oz. apricot brandy
    2 dashes grenadine
    7-up or Sprite to fill

Boston Cooler
    2 oz. rum
    ½ oz. sour mix
    soda or ginger ale to fill
Garnish with a lemon twist (extra long spiral) and an orange
slice. This is a fizzier version of the rum Collins.

Gin Cooler/Vodka Cooler
Substitute the appropriate liquor for rum in the Boston Cooler.

Rum Cooler
   3 oz. rum
   ¹/₂ oz. lemon juice
   3 oz. pineapple juice
   tonic water to fill

Scotch Cooler
   2 oz. Scotch
   splash crème de menthe
   soda water to fill
Garnish with mint sprigs.

Tequooler (Tequila Cooler)
   1¹/₂ oz. tequila
   juice of ¹/₂ lemon or lime
   tonic water or soda water to fill
Garnish with a lemon twist (extra long spiral).

: X. BEER DRINKS :

Are you the kind of connoisseur whose favorite cocktail is a beer straight from the can? You'll be amazed at what you can do with your old standby.

HALF-AND-HALFS

Serve these drinks in a beer mug or Pilsner glass.

Black Velvet
   1 part porter or stout
   1 part champagne (extra dry)

Pour these carefully down the side of the glass to make two distinct layers.

Half-and-Half
    1 part ale
    1 part porter or stout
In all, 10 to 16 ounces.

Shandy Gaff
    1 part beer
    1 part ginger ale
In all, 10 to 16 ounces.

BEER DRINKS

Boilermaker
To a mug of beer, add a jigger of whiskey. You can (a) drink the whiskey and chase it with the beer (boring), (b) pour the shot into the beer (better), or (c) drop the shot—glass and all—into the mug of beer and chug it all down quickly before it foams all over you. This is somtimes called a "depth charge."
    Beer and whiskey, mighty risky!

Sneaky Pete
To a mug of beer, add a jigger of applejack.

Hop-Skip-and-Go-Naked
   1 oz. vodka
   1 oz. gin
   juice of ½ lime
   beer to fill
Serve over ice. To serve as a punch, measure the ingredients
by the bottle and case.

: XI. SHOTS :

Alabama Slammer
See page 65.

Honolulu Hammer
See page 65.

Kamikaze
Make a pitcher as follows:
   3 parts vodka
   1 part triple sec
   1 part Rose's lime juice
Optional: top with 7-up or Sprite. Kamikazes closely resemble
the highball known as the "Orgasm," but, unlike the Orgasm,
should always be taken in shots. (See page 44.)

Laser Beam
  1 part peppermint schnapps
  1 part Galliano
  1 part Drambuie
  1 part bourbon
Shake with ice and strain into shot glasses.

Tequila Shot
1. Lick the left hand in the crook between the thumb and forefinger. Sprinkle salt on the back of that area.
2. Hold a shot of tequila between the thumb and forefinger.
3. Hold a wedge of lemon in the right hand.

Then, in a smooth, swift motion:

4. Lick the salt.
5. Down the shot.
6. Suck the lemon.
7. Smile.

As a variation, some people prefer to salt the right hand so they can lick the salt off without spilling the shot. Choose your method based on your own coordination.

:4:

Group Therapy
The Cocktail Party

Let's pause a moment and evaluate your progress. Technically, you are no longer a Problem Drinkmaker: you can recite every term defined in chapter 1, describe exactly how to prepare the drinks in chapter 2, and you've memorized all the recipes in chapter 3 (even the really obscure ones that you will probably never hear of again). Cured? Be honest with yourself. Nobody tends bar using brain power alone. So drop that façade, relinquish that stubborn pride—and ask your friends for help. You need group therapy. Like it or not, now it's time to throw a cocktail party for your friends and practice *on them* everything you've memorized.

Don't worry. They're your friends, aren't they? Friends will understand if your drinks don't taste quite right the first time—in fact, they probably won't even notice. And remember, you've got eleven years of Harvard Bartending School experience here to help you.

This book may never leave your hand during the week before your first cocktail party. As the party date approaches and you begin to panic, you'll wonder . . .

● How much liquor and mixer should I buy? What kinds? How much ice? Where can I find enough glasses for this many guests?

98

- How do I set up a cocktail party bar? Where should I put it? What should I do if I run out of supplies during the party.
- Can I serve punch at my party? What are some good punch recipes?
- How can I suggest that guests leave when it gets late (without resorting to rudeness or physical force)? Uncle Ed and Aunt Mary always drink too much—should I let them drive home?
- How will I ever clean up the mess?

Do these questions sound familiar? Then, by all means, read on.

Preparation—Ordering Supplies

You've probably witnessed this scene before: A Problem Drinkmaker decides to throw a party without any help, saunters overconfidently into the liquor store to place a complex order, and *thud*—faints dead away from the sheer intimidation of all those different liquors, brands, and bottle sizes. Another victim of "selection shock" bites the dust. Fortunately, this condition isn't serious; the application of some sensible, practical liquor selection advice usually revives the patient in minutes.

Even the worst selection shock victims understand the simple, basic bar. The basic bar includes:

- At least two kinds of light alcohol: gin and vodka (usually rum as well; sometimes tequila)
- At least two kinds of dark alcohol: Scotch and bourbon (usually also blended whiskey)
- Two vermouths: dry and sweet
- Wine: white (sometimes also red, rosé, and fortified)
- Beer

For a typical four-hour cocktail party, plan on one one-liter bottle of liquor for every six guests. (Make sure you buy the one-liter size because it's easiest to handle. Larger bottles may cost less per drink, but they're bulky, heavy, and usually won't take speedpourers. Also, unless you're giving an informal party at home, think twice before buying large bottles and pouring the liquor into smaller containers: this "marrying" of bottles is illegal in many states.) You will need only one bottle of each vermouth. One bottle of dry vermouth should suffice, not just for one party, but for your whole life.

Five variables will influence your liquor selection decisions:

> *Season:* In warm weather, people tend to order light alcohols, beer, and white wine. Conversely, in winter, stock up on dark alcohols, coffee drinks (such as Irish Coffee and Mexican Coffee), sherry, brandy, and red wine.

> *Age:* Younger people usually prefer light alcohol, blended drinks, wine, beer, and sweet-tasting liqueur cocktails. Older guests drink more dark alcohols, usually unmixed. Buy the highest quality, most prestigious brands you can afford for older, whiskey-drinking guests. They will expect and recognize better names.

Theme or holiday: If the party theme or a holiday season lends itself to special drinks, alter your bar's offerings accordingly. Serve eggnog, hot mulled wine, or punch at a Christmas party; champagne on New Year's Eve; mint juleps on Kentucky Derby day; a red or pink "love potion" punch on Valentine's Day; and green-colored beer on St. Patrick's Day. If a friend just won a sailing race, serve Sea Breezes. The day before you leave for a trip to Greece, celebrate with ouzo (and set three alarm clocks).

Time of day: At a ten A.M. brunch bar, don't expect to be making many Zombies, or even gin and tonics. Instead, concentrate on mimosas, screwdrivers, and Bloody Marys. Before dinner, serve light aperitifs— drinks to stimulate appetites, not anesthetize them: for instance, wine, light cocktails, Dubonnet, and kir. As a general rule, add more liquor and more variety as the day progresses, culminating with a fully-stocked bar for the eight P.M. to two A.M. crowd.

Guests' preferences: Use your own judgement for other bar adjustments. If your best friend drinks only sombreros, keep a bottle of Kahlúa at the bar. Consider also that trends these days lean toward an overall preference for light alcohol and sweet drinks.

Confused about brand name selection? Two factors should govern which brands you buy: your budget and your desire to impress the guests. If you have money growing on trees in

your yard and you're coordinating a party for the boss and the new clients, buy top-shelf liquor (the name brands considered the highest quality, and usually the most expensive). On a more limited budget for a party with the neighbors, you can get by with middle-shelf brands (good-quality, recognizable brands, but usually cheaper than top-shelf). For a fraternity party or for use in a punch, buy bottom-shelf or generic liquor—these guests probably won't be scrutinizing labels. They won't care about it.

If you must economize, buy cheaper brands among your light alcohols; they usually go into mixed drinks, so guests can't taste subtle brand differences. Then you can spend more on the higher quality dark alcohols, which people often drink unmixed. For example, at that party for the new clients, you could do well with Smirnoff vodka instead of a top-shelf import—a good name brand at a more reasonable price.

Still confused about liquor quality and brand selection? Read chapter 5 before you place any liquor orders.

If you want to economize even further without sacrificing name-brand prestige, consider mixing weaker drinks. Make a 1¼-ounce- or a 1-ounce-based highball and the liquor bottles won't empty as quickly.

Make sure when you order for a large party to specify in advance that you want to buy on consignment. "On consignment" means you can return any unopened, *sealed* bottles for a refund after the party. Sometimes this option costs a little more, but it can be worth it. Ask for details at your liquor store.

In addition to the hard stuff, beer and wine are important additions to your bar. (Alter the suggested amounts that follow according to the age of your guests: buy more beer and wine for a young crowd, less for older folks.)

For a standard, four-hour cocktail party, plan on about one case of beer for every ten guests. Buying cans will allow you to store them in any available ice supply without worrying about breakage. At 35 guests or more, consider purchasing a quarter-keg (about 7.8 gallons—the equivalent of almost 3.5 cases, or 83 12-ounce servings). For 70 guests, buy a keg (technically a half-keg, which contains 15.5 gallons—about 7 cases, or 165 12-ounce servings). Keg beer is economical in the long run, but you will have to leave a deposit on the keg and tap—don't break or lose them. For the best-tasting beer, move the keg to its party location well ahead of time and keep it consistently cold until empty. Put it in a big tub or barrel, pack chunks of ice around it (try for block ice, which won't melt as fast as cubed or cocktail ice), and cover it with a big plastic bag or towel. Try to get a pressure-tap keg (which dispenses from the top) rather than a gravity keg (with the tap near the bottom), because the latter is hard to keep cold.

To tap a keg, first remove the plastic cap from the top. Then, place the tap on the outlet and turn the ring clockwise to screw it onto the keg. Pump the tap to pressurize the keg and open the faucet to drain out the first few foamy beers. During the party, whenever the stream of beer weakens, just pump the tap a few times to repressurize the keg. Some tap systems work quite differently from this one, however, so make sure you ask for instructions at the liquor store when you pick up your keg.

Let the season, the guests' ages, and your budget dictate quantity and kinds of wine to order for your party. Warm weather and a young crowd usually require a lot of white wine. In winter and with older folks, wine consumption decreases; you may want to serve some red or fortified wines, brandy, or sherry to take the chill out of the air. Running low on funds? Just buy white and try to get a case discount—ask your liquor or wine salesman for advice on purchasing a cheap, rather dry, white wine.

Wine comes in bottles containing 750 milliliters, 1.5 or 3 liters, a magnum (52 ounces), a jeroboam (104 ounces), a rehoboam (156 ounces), and, for your wildest bacchanalian orgies, a jeromagnum (208 ounces). Buy whatever size costs the least. Transfer wine from large bottles to carafes for serving ease and attractiveness.

The amount you will need varies from party to party. One case of wine contains 70 4-ounce servings, so assess your needs based on that formula. A heavy wine-drinking group may consume three glasses per person, whereas an older crowd gathered during cold weather would drink only half a glass per person.

Now, with all the liquor logistics so carefully planned, you will need something to mix with it. If you ordered more light liquors, buy lots of tonic water and some cola and fruit juices: plan on 2 quarts of these mixers to each liter of light alcohol. Whiskey drinkers won't want much added to their liquor, so buy only 1 quart of soda water, ginger ale, Sprite, or 7-up for each liter of dark alcohol. Don't forget diet soda for your sugar-conscious guests.

Many people—even normal, non–Problem Drinkmakers—underestimate the most important cocktail ingredient: ice. Sure, liquor is a crucial part of any alcoholic beverage, but if you run out of blended whiskey or gin, guests can at least switch to something else. But what happens when all the ice melts away? For a typical, four-hour party, plan on 1 pound of ice per person. In winter, you could get away with only ¾ pound, and in summer you should buy 1½ pounds per guest. If you want to fill an ice chest for beer and wine, remember to get enough to fill the chest in addition to cocktail ice needs.

Now don't start trying to figure out how many freezers you should buy so you can make and store all that ice. Instead, check the Yellow Pages for an ice house nearby where you can order ice in quantity (by the 40-pound bag, for instance). Some places will deliver right to your home on the day of the party. One word of caution—make sure to specify *cocktail ice* when you order so you won't have to hand-chop each cube off a 40-pound *block*.

You will also want some garnishes to enhance the taste and appearance of the cocktails. For the basic bar, cut up in advance: lime wedges (one lime for every six guests—more for a young crowd and more in the summer); lemon twists and a few lemon slices (one lemon for every 50 people); and perhaps some orange slices (one orange for every 25 people— this one's optional). Also consider buying a jar each of olives (a must for martinis), onions (optional—only if you're inviting a Gibson drinker), and cherries (for Manhattans). Fruit-cutting instructions and additional suggestions are in chapter 1.

The basic bartending kit described in chapter 1 and on page 204 should take care of your utensil needs. Also make sure you have at least one trash barrel, a large ice bucket, a sharp knife for cutting fruit, a water pitcher, a towel, and an ashtray for the bar. Ashtrays seem pretty insignificant sometimes, don't they? Here you are, a Problem Drinkmaker, and you're expected to remember a silly ashtray? Caution: Smokers waiting for a drink will notice the missing ashtray. They tend to find substitute ashtrays such as carpets, upholstered chairs, other peoples' drinks, your lime wedge dish, a trouser cuff . . .

Remember to put out some cocktail napkins for your guests. For a nice touch, place the stack of napkins on the bar, put a shot glass in the center, and bear down firmly as you twist the glass clockwise. Remove the glass and you've created a pretty, fanned design of cocktail napkins.

Of course, you'll need something to serve your masterpieces in. Although your best glasses may look absolutely gorgeous, some of them probably won't survive the rigors of a party. Instead, opt for "plassware," disposable plastic glasses, which are perfectly acceptable for even some of the fanciest gatherings. You need only two types: the lowball or on-the-rocks cup, which is short and wide and holds about 9 ounces, and the highball cup which is taller and holds 10 to 12 ounces. Into the highball you'll pour the popular highballs, beers, and Collinses, and into the lowball will go virtually everything else—stirred cocktails, many shaken drinks, on-the-rocks liquor, and wine. For a four-hour party, buy at least two cups per person, at a ratio of 75 percent highball to 25 percent lowball. For a dance party, plan on at least three cups per person; people tend to put the cups down to dance and then forget about them.

If you insist on real glasses, check the phone book for a general rental agency. Some will even deliver the glasses to your home and pick them up again after the party.

Setting Up the Bar

Once you collect all these supplies, you'll need to set them up on the bar in an efficient, orderly arrangement. The bar itself can be just a table that is strong enough to hold all those bottles. Cover it with a plastic tablecloth for protection from spills, with a linen tablecloth over that if you're going fancy.

For small parties (less than 15 people), you don't need a bartender. A self-service bar, set up like the one shown here, provides room for two guests to mix their own drinks.

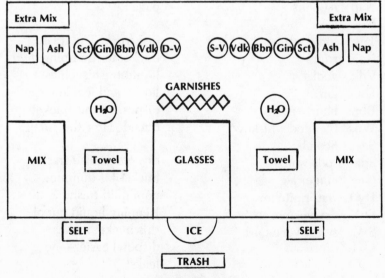

Self-Service Bar

KEY

Nap	napkins	Vdk	vodka
Ash	ashtray	D-V	dry vermouth
Sct	Scotch	S-V	sweet vermouth
Gin	gin	H₂O	water pitcher
Bbn	bourbon		

Parties of 20 to 100 people tend to run more smoothly with the help of a bartender. The diagrams at right illustrate two possible setups for one-man bars.

KEY

Ash	ashtray
Nap	napkins
Col	cola
Tnc	tonic water
Rum	rum
Vdk	vodka
Gin	gin
Bbn	bourbon
Whs	blended whiskey
Sct	Scotch
Sda	soda water
Gng	ginger ale
H₂O	water pitcher
D-V	dry vermouth
S-V	sweet vermouth

"show" bottle (see page 2)

wet trash: The trash bucket for dumping *only* liquid trash such as liquor and ice. You can dispose of this bucket outside after the party.

dry trash: The trash bucket for dumping nonliquid trash. Keeping liquid out of this bucket makes disposal easier—no leaks!

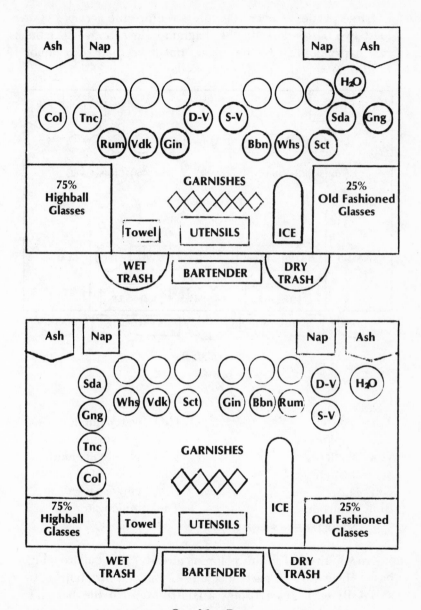

One-Man Bars

Large parties of over 100 guests require the services of at least two bartenders. In the diagram below, notice that the two bartenders share the mixers but have their own liquor bottles for speed and efficiency's sake.

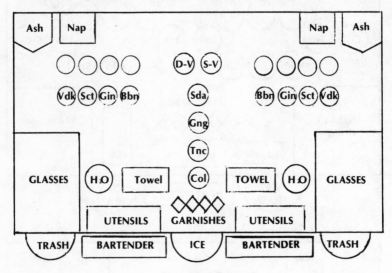

Two-Man Bar

KEY

Ash	ashtray	H₂O	water pitcher
Nap	napkins	D-V	dry vermouth
Vdk	vodka	S-V	sweet vermouth
Sct	Scotch	Sda	soda water
Gin	gin	Gng	ginger ale
Bbn	bourbon	Tnc	tonic water
	show bottle (see page 2)	Col	cola

Are you tired of all this planning already? Can't afford a big bash? Have a BYOB party instead—bring your own bottle. At a BYOB, each guest brings a contribution to the bar. It's impossible to diagram a BYOB setup as it can get pretty confusing, so you'll just have to improvise.

Use common sense in setting up the party room. The most efficient bar arrangement in the world becomes worthless if you place it next to a doorway where it can be clogged up by crowded party traffic. Put the bar away from the door, preferably against a wall so guests cannot sneak up behind you and pour their own drinks. If this happens, your bar will suddenly lose its wonderful, carefully planned efficiency. You might reach for a bottle and either find it's not there, or inadvertently pour the wrong liquor into a drink.

Working the Party

It's time. You've meticulously planned, plotted, ordered, and arranged every detail. The guests arrive—just a few at first, but then more and more of them. Suddenly, you're tending bar! Pouring, mixing, shaking, and straining. Sometimes the line gets pretty long, but you just keep moving and eventually bring the situation under control. No problem.

Although you're doing fine, perhaps a few suggestions from the pros might make things run a bit more smoothly. First and foremost, *never* leave the bar, or your lovely arrangement will look like a tornado struck it by the time you return. Cocktail party guests won't wait while you run to the kitchen for more ice and mixers.

The second important rule is a little trickier to manage: Keep the bar supplied. But if you can't leave the bar, how can you stay fully stocked? If you run out of ice or mixers, guests might leave! When you notice something running low, ask a co-worker, the host, or a friend to get it for you when he or she gets a chance. If you're working alone and can't find the host, improvise. Look for that bratty little son of the host who has been allowed to stay up way past his bedtime and is fascinated by your bartending abilities. Or what about that lonely-looking guest hanging out by the bar who just doesn't seem to fit in with everyone else. These two would probably love to fetch more ice for you.

If it bothers you to have a line of guests waiting for drinks at the bar, put out a dish of peanuts or pretzels for them to munch on while they wait. Snacks will keep people occupied for a few minutes during a busy period.

On the other hand, if the bar slows down and you find yourself with nothing to do, keep busy. Pick up empty cups, dirty napkins, and straws. Wipe spills. Empty the trash and ashtrays. If you keep the bar area relatively tidy during the party, clean-up will be much easier at the end of the night.

For more hints on how to look like a pro behind the bar, read chapter 7. There, you'll find suggestions for proper appearance, attitude, and behavior, and how to find cocktail party jobs. One professional perquisite discussed in chapter 7 calls for some clarification here: tips. At a private party, a tip cup on the bar looks dreadfully tacky. On the other hand, if you work at a rather "impersonal" party, such as a large company gathering or some sort of dance, guests may want to reward you for extra-special service. In those cases, ask the person who hired you if you can put a tip cup out (and then put a dollar in it to give guests a hint).

Punch Recipes

So you're still a little shy about pouring in public? Try some of these punch recipes so you can show off your new bartending abilities while still mixing in the privacy of your own home.

All the following recipes should be served from a punch bowl with a large block of ice in it, unless directions specify otherwise. For each serving, ladle about 4 ounces into a plastic lowball glass.

Brandy Punch
Mix:
   juice of 1 dozen lemons
   juice of 4 oranges
Add sugar to taste. Mix with:
   1 cup grenadine
   1 cup triple sec
   2 liters five-star brandy
   2 cups tea (optional)
   1 quart soda water
Add soda water just before serving. Garnish with fruit.
Yields 35–50 servings.

Buddha Punch
   1 bottle Rhine wine
   ½ cup curaçao
   ½ cup rum
   1 cup orange juice
   1 quart soda water
   Angostura bitters to taste
   1 bottle champagne
Add champagne just before serving. Garnish with mint leaves and fruit slices.
Yields 25–30 servings.

Note: One bottle of wine or champagne usually equals 750 ml or one quart. Either size is acceptable.

Canadian Fruit Punch
    2 liters Canadian Whiskey
    1 12 oz. can frozen orange juice
    1 12 oz. can frozen lemonade
    1 12 oz. can frozen pineapple juice
    1 cup simple syrup (see recipe on page 16)
    3 quarts strong tea
Garnish with fruit.
Yields 65–75 servings.

Champagne Punches—see page 122

Claret Punch
    2 bottles Claret (or a 1.5 liter bottle)
    ½ cup curaçao
    1 cup simple syrup (see recipe on page 16)
    1 cup lemon juice
    1 pint orange juice
    ½ cup pineapple juice
    2 quarts club soda
Add club soda just before serving.
Yields about 40 servings.

Eggnog
    1 pint brandy
    1 pint light rum
    12 eggs, separated
    1 lb. confectioner's sugar
    1½ quarts milk
    1 pint heavy cream
Beat confectioner's sugar in with egg *yolks*. Stir in slowly:
brandy, rum, milk, and cream. Chill. Then fold in stiffly beaten
egg whites before serving. Do *not* serve with ice. Sprinkle
nutmeg on top.
Yields 45–65 servings.

Fish House Punch
  1 liter rum
  1 750 ml. bottle brandy
  1/2 cup peach brandy
  2–3 quarts cola or lemonade or another flavored soda
Garnish with citrus fruits.
Yields 25–35 servings.

French Cream Punch
  1 cup amaretto
  1 cup Kahlúa or coffee brandy
  1/4 cup triple sec
  1/2 gallon softened French vanilla ice cream
No ice. Mix well.
Yields 15–20 servings.

Fruit Punch
  1 liter vodka
  1 bottle white wine
  2 12 oz. cans frozen concentrate fruit juice (pineapple, grape-
    fruit, orange)
  2 quarts club soda
Add club soda just before serving.
Yields about 40 servings.

Gin Punch
  2 liters gin
  1 pint lemon juice
  2 cups cranberry juice cocktail
  1 quart orange juice
  1/2 cup grenadine
  1 quart club soda
Add club soda just before serving. Garnish with sprigs
of mint.
Yields about 45 servings.

Green Machine
    2 liters vodka
    1½ gallons limeade concentrate
    ½ pint lemon sherbet
    ½ pint lime sherbet
Yields about 35 servings.

Hot Apple Rum Punch
    1 liter dark rum
    1 quart apple cider
    2 or 3 cinnamon sticks, broken
    1½ tbsp. butter
Heat in saucepan until almost boiling. Serve hot.
Yields about 15 servings.

Hot Mulled Wine
    2 cups water
    2 cinnamon sticks, whole
    8 cloves
    peel of 1 lemon, cut into twists or into one long spiral
    ¼ cup simple syrup (see recipe on page 16)
Boil together in large saucepan for 10 minutes. Add 2 bottles
of dry red wine. Heat but do not allow to boil. To each glass,
just before serving, add a splash of cognac and a lemon slice.
Serve hot.
Yields 15–25 servings.

Oogie Pringle Punch
    1 liter rum
    1 quart pineapple juice
    1 quart cranberry juice
Garnish with lemon slices.
Yields about 25 servings.

Party Punch
Boil for 5 minutes:
  2 cups sugar
  1 cup water
Add:
  2 cups concentrated fruit syrup
  1 cup lemon juice
  2 cups orange juice
  2 cups pineapple juice
Just before serving, add:
  2 bottles champagne
  2 quarts ginger ale
  1 quart soda water
Yields about 55 servings.

Planter's Punch
  1 liter rum
  1 pint Jamaican rum (Myers's)
  1 pint lime juice
  1 pint simple syrup (see recipe on page 16)
  1 quart soda water
Add soda water just before serving. Garnish with orange slices and cherries.
Yields about 30 servings.

Planter's Punch (variation)
  1 liter rum
  1 cup Jamaican rum (Myers's)
  1 cup curaçao (optional)
  1 pint lemon juice
  1 cup orange juice
  1 cup pineapple juice
Garnish with orange slices and cherries.
Yields about 20 servings.

Red Wine Punch
    2 bottles red Bordeaux wine
    1 pint lemon juice
    1 cup simple syrup (see recipe on page 16)
    1 cup raspberry syrup
    2 quarts club soda
Add soda water just before serving.
Yields about 40 servings.

Rum Fruit Punch
    1½ liters rum
    ½ pineapple, sliced
    1 pint strawberries
    ¾ cup simple syrup (see recipe on page 16)
    1 cup lemon juice
    2 cups pineapple juice
Chill for 2 hours. Just before serving, add:
    1 pint thinly sliced strawberries
    2 quarts soda water
Yields 40–45 servings.

Sangria
    2 bottles rosé wine
    1 cup rum
    2 cups orange juice
    2 cups pineapple juice
    1 quart ginger ale
    1 30 oz. can fruit cocktail
    3 sliced oranges
Yields 35–40 servings.

Sangria Maria
Blend together:
    1 jug hearty Burgundy wine (1.5 liters)
    1 quart ginger ale
Cut up, squeeze, drop in:

4 oranges
2 lemons
2 peaches
any other fruits you wish to add
Let stand at least 2 hours. Strain into punch bowl with ice.
Garnish with fresh lemon and orange slices and cherries.
Yields about 25 servings.

Narri's Sangria
This delicious Sangria recipe comes from the bar of Narri, the
manager of the Harvard Bartending Course.
   Soak fruit (strawberries, oranges, lemons, limes, and whatever else is available) overnight in:
   2 cups dark rum
Add:
   1 quart sweet red wine
   1 quart dry red wine
Yields 25–30 servings.

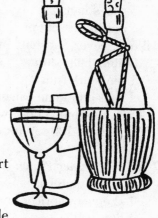

Southern Comfort Punch
   1 750 ml. bottle Southern Comfort
   2 cups grapefruit juice
   1 cup lemon juice
   2 quarts 7-up, Sprite, or ginger ale
Yields about 30 servings.

Sparkling Pink Punch
Pour
   1 bottle champagne
   1 bottle rosé wine
over:
   1 10 oz. container thawed whole frozen raspberries
      or strawberries
Yields about 15 servings.

Tequila Punch
 1 liter tequila
 4 bottles sauterne
 2 quarts fruit cubes and balls (8 cups)
 1 bottle champagne
Sweeten to taste. Add champagne just before serving.
Yields about 45 servings.

Tropical Punch
 5 bottles white wine
 1 lb. brown sugar
 1 quart orange juice
 1 pint lemon juice
 5 sliced bananas
 1 pineapple, cut or chopped
Blend, cover, let stand overnight. Add:
 3 liters light rum
 1 pint dark rum
 2 cups crème de banana
Strain into punch bowl with ice. Garnish with fruits.
Yields about 100 servings.

Velvet Hammer Punch
 1 bottle sauterne
 1–2 ounces apricot brandy
 1 liter vodka
 1 bottle champagne
 1 quart ginger ale
Add champagne and ginger ale just before serving.
Yields about 30 servings

Wedding Punch
 1 liter vodka
 3 cups orange juice
 1 cup lemon juice
 2 quarts ginger ale

Garnish with cherries, lemon and orange slices.
Yields about 35 servings.

Welders' Punch
    1 liter vodka
    1 quart ginger ale, 7-up, or Sprite
    1 quart fruit punch
    1 quart orange juice
Garnish with orange slices and cherries.
Yields about 35 servings.

Whiskey Punch
    2 liters bourbon
    ½ cup curaçao
    1 quart apple juice
    juice of 6 lemons
    2 ounces grenadine
    4 quarts ginger ale
Add ginger ale just before serving. Garnish with cherries.
Yields 60–65 servings.

Wine Punch
Dissolve:
    1½ lbs. sugar
in:
    2 quarts soda water
Add:
    2 bottles Claret
    1 pint brandy
    1 pint rum
Garnish with a sliced orange and several slices of pineapple.
Just before serving, add:
    1 bottle sparkling white wine
Yields 45–50 servings.

Champagne Punch
　2 or 3 bottles champagne
　½ cup curaçao
　½ cup lemon juice
　1 quart soda water
　½ lb. confectioner's sugar
Mix this punch just before serving.
Yields 25–35 servings.

Champagne Punch
　½ cup brandy
　½ cup Cointreau or triple sec
　2 bottles champagne
Yields about 15 servings.

Champagne Punch
　½ cup light rum
　½ cup dark rum
　juice of 2 lemons
　juice of 2 oranges
　1 cup pineapple juice
　½ cup sugar
　2 bottles champagne
Add champagne just before serving.
Yields about 20 servings.

Champagne Punch
Slice and arrange in bottom of punch bowl:
　6 oranges
Sprinkle with sugar. Pour over fruit:
　1 bottle Moselle wine
Let stand at least one hour. Just before serving, place ice
block in bowl and add 4 bottles champagne.
Yields about 30 servings.

Champagne Holiday Punch
   1 bottle champagne
   2 quarts ginger ale
   1 8 oz. can crushed pineapple with juice
   1 quart raspberry sherbet
Mix this punch just before serving.
Yields 25–35 servings.

Champagne Rum Punch
   2 liters rum
   1 bottle sweet vermouth (750 ml.)
   1 quart orange juice
   1 bottle champagne
Add champagne just before serving. Garnish with sliced bananas.
Yields about 40 servings.

Champagne Sherbet Punch
   1 quart lemon or pineapple sherbet
   2 bottles champagne
   1 bottle sauterne
Put sherbet in first. Garnish with lemon slices and/or pineapple chunks.
Yields about 25 servings.

NONALCOHOLIC PUNCHES

Fruit Punch
Dilute two to one with water:
  1 large can frozen grape juice (16 oz.)
  1 large can frozen lemonade (16 oz.)
  1 large can frozen orange juice (16 oz.)
Add before serving:
  1 quart ginger ale
Spoon 1 pint raspberry sherbet over punch before serving.
Garnish with orange slices and strawberries.
Yields 45–50 servings.

Snoopy Punch
  1 large can frozen lemonade (16 oz.)
  1 large can frozen fruit punch (16 oz.)
  1 pint pineapple sherbet
  3 lemons, sliced
  1 quart ginger ale
Add ginger ale just before serving. If you serve this punch to
anyone over 12, you may want to give it a different name.
Yields about 40 servings.

If you aren't thrilled with any of these punch recipes, try
converting your favorite highball into punch form. For example, a Sea Breeze contains:

  1½ ounces vodka
  2 ounces grapefruit juice (approximately)
  2 ounces cranberry juice (approximately)

In punch form, this would loosely translate into:

  1 liter vodka
  2 quarts grapefruit juice
  2 quarts cranberry juice

This recipe would make a delicious, beautiful, cool summer punch. Adapt the ingredients to suit your tastes—add more mixer or more vodka to vary the alcohol content.

The Party's Over?

Are you getting a bit tired? Supplies starting to run low? Ready to call it a night? But the guests show *no* sign of leaving? To prod people gently toward the door, start putting the bar away. Pack up extra liquor and mixers and bring them out to the kitchen. Then take speedpourers out of the remaining bottles, put the caps on and put those bottles away. Eventually, guests will notice the absence of liquor and start heading home.

Did Uncle Ed and Aunt Mary drink too much again? Tsk, tsk. Do *not* let them stumble out to the car and try to drive home. Either ask another guest to drop them off, call a cab, or give them each a cup of coffee to sip until you get a chance to bring them home. Party hosts *can* be sued for damages caused by drunken guests, so protect yourself and the people you serve.

Party Checklist

The following list offers suggestions, ideas, and reminders. Of course, you shouldn't run out and buy everything on this list! Consider your guests' preferences and choose accordingly:

Equipment

shaker glass	corkscrew/bottle opener/can opener
shaker shell	ashtrays
strainer	bar napkins
jigger	water pitcher
speedpourers	dry and wet trash buckets
bar spoon	swizzle sticks/cocktail straws
ice bucket	

Liquor

bourbon   tequila
blended whiskey   beer
Scotch   wine
vodka   dry vermouth
gin   sweet vermouth
rum   other liquors?

Mixers

tonic water   Bloody Mary mix
cola   mixing juices
soda water   light cream
ginger ale   milk
Sprite or 7-up   water
diet soda   Rose's lime juice
sour mix

Glassware (plastic)

lowball   beer
highball   wine

Garbage/Garnishes

lemon twists and slices specialty garnishes (optional)
lime wedges   stemmed maraschino cherries
orange slices   cocktail onions
                           olives

Condiments

bitters   Bloody Mary condiments:
bar sugar   Tabasco sauce
nutmeg   Worcestershire sauce
salt   salt and pepper
grenadine   horseradish

Ordering Summary

If all those ordering formulas scattered throughout the chapter have confused you, use this quick summary as a reminder.

Liquor: 1 liter per 6 guests
Mixer: 2 quarts per each liter light alcohol
　　　　 1 quart per each liter dark alcohol
Ice: ¾ pound per person—winter
　　　 1 pound per person—moderate weather
　　　 1½ pounds per person—summer
　　　 More as needed to fill wine and beer chest
Garnish: 1 lime per 6 people (more in summer and
　　　　　　　for young people)
　　　　 1 lemon per 50 people
　　　　 1 orange per 25 people (optional)
Glasses: 2 per person (more for dance party)
　　　　 75% highball
　　　　 25% lowball

Putting it all together—
A Sample Party

Poor Babs. A lifelong Problem Drinkmaker, she never took the time to enroll in the Harvard Bartending Course, clinging to the hope that nobody would notice her social handicap (not a good idea). One day, she appeared at the Harvard Bartending office—in tears—and asked for emergency "first aid" treatment. A co-worker had just been transferred to the company's Mexican office, and Babs was assigned the monumental task of planning the going-away party.

She scheduled the party for a Thursday night in late June from seven to eleven o'clock. Seventy-five people planned to attend; their ages ranged from 23 to 65 years old, with most in their mid-thirties.

One hour after she arrived, Babs left the Harvard Bartending offices with a huge smile on her face and one precious piece of paper clasped in her hand. The paper read as follows:

Liquor: 13 bottles (1 liter each)

3 Smirnoff vodka ⎫ (These lights cost less than
3 Gordon's gin ⎬ expensive imports, but have
1 Bacardi rum ⎭ very well-respected names)
1 Chivas Regal Scotch (Because the boss likes
            Chivas.)

1 Seagrams VO
1 Early Times Bourbon
2 José Cuervo tequila ⎫ (Margaritas will be the
1 triple sec   ⎭ Mexican theme drink.)

1 sweet vermouth (750 ml)
1 dry vermouth (750 ml)

1 keg Michelob (Technically, a half-keg.
           Michelob not as expensive
           as imports—good domestic
           beer.)

2 cases white wine (Whatever is on sale at the
           store.)

Mixers: (quart bottles)

7 tonic water
3 cola
3 soda (In hot weather, buy *lots* of
3 ginger ale mixers, especially for light
2 diet sodas liquors.)
3 grapefruit juice
3 cranberry juice
5 orange juice
1 Bloody Mary mix
1 Rose's lime juice

Ice:
4 40-pound bags cocktail ice (3 for drinks, 1 for wine chest)
large block of ice for keg barrel

Plastic glassware: (Get the disposable kind that comes in stacks of about 25 per package.)
150 highball glasses
50 lowball glasses

Garnishes:
30 limes (1 per 5 people in hot weather, plus 15 more for Margaritas)
2 lemons
jar olives
jar maraschino cherries
grenadine (for tequila sunrises)
salt (for Margaritas)

Equipment:
bar kit and extra speedpourers
knife for cutting fruit
2 trashbarrels (one for the keg)
ice chest for wine
water pitcher
paper towels

Other supplies:
cocktail straws and napkins

Still nervous about coordinating your own "group therapy" session? Look, if Babs could do it, *you* certainly can. So go ahead—enjoy the party! With the help of friends, you might just become the best bartender on your block.

:5:

The Root of the Problem
Alcohol

A businessman wrestles with a 42-percent sales decrease . . . A doctor works feverishly around the clock, unable to isolate the cause of a mysterious disease . . . A computer programmer spends weeks trying to locate the one little error that prevents her program from running . . . *You* cannot mix a drink . . .

What do all of these frustrated people have in common? Twelve anguished words: "Aaarghh! If only I could get to the *root* of the problem!"

As with the businessman's product defect, the doctor's virus, and the computer programmer's syntax error on line 226, if you could get to the root of your drinkmaking problem, maybe you'd solve everything.

What causes Problem Drinkmaking? Perhaps you are the one at fault for not learning to mix drinks earlier in life. One could accuse your parents for neglecting to teach you proper bar etiquette during your formative years. What about society? The American educational system?

No. Dig deeper, into the *real* root of it all. That's right—if *alcohol* were never invented, you would never have become a Problem Drinkmaker.

Alas, alcohol was indeed invented, but if you could learn more about it, you might just become a better bartender. Read this chapter and find out about what you're trying to mix, including:

- What alcohol is, technically speaking
- A brief history of liquor
- How whiskies, gin, vodka, rum and tequila are made
- What determines liquor quality
- What all those liqueurs, brandies, and infrequently used liquors on the back bar *are*
- Some basics about beer and wine

What *is* alcohol?

Liquor contains *ethyl* alcohol (ethanol), as opposed to methyl (wood) or isopropyl (rubbing) alcohols. Technically, it forms as the product of a chemical reaction in which yeast enzymes decompose carbohydrates into CO_2 and C_2H_5OH. In plain English, that means a grain- or fruit-and-yeast culture will generate ethyl alcohol and carbon dioxide (bubbles). The carbon dioxide can be left in the alcohol, as in beer, or allowed to evaporate into the atmosphere.

A Spirited History

Now Noah began to till the soil and he planted a vineyard. When he drank of the wine he became drunk.

—Gen. 9:20–21

Some things in life are ageless, aren't they? (As a matter of fact, Noah lived 350 years after that binge.) Early references in literature and historical documents indicate that alcohol in one form or another has been around for a very long time in most cultures. Many bartenders find this history interesting and very useful; they can impress friends and customers with obscure liquor knowledge, and thus earn bigger tips. Aren't you curious to find out how this whole business of alcohol and bartending evolved?

Dates and details remain sketchy, but researchers believe that primitive agricultural societies enjoyed the first tastes of alcohol. Apparently, these people chewed grain and spat it out; enzymes in the saliva converted grain starch to sugar, which fermented into alcohol.

Other early societies found more palatable ways to turn carbohydrates into beverages. Between approximately 1000 B.C. and 1000 A.D., people of Asian lands made alcohol from rice and mare's milk. The English fermented honey to produce mead, a wine which is still made commercially in England and Denmark (so if you're really curious, it's not too late to try it). The Italians, French, and Spanish produced grape wine, and the Irish fermented an oat-and-barley malt to make beer.

Eventually, the Scotch and Irish began producing *uisge beatha* or *usquebaugh* from their beer. This Gaelic word, meaning "water of life," has evolved into today's word for the liquor: whiskey. To make whiskey, the Celts distilled beer; that is, they took some of the water out of it.

Soon after, a French shipmaster discovered another product of distillation when he tried to make wine easier to ship (or so the story goes). He imagined that he should be able to take water out of his wine, ship the alcohol part alone, and then later put the water back into the wine. To do this, he heated wine to a temperature between 78°C. (at which alcohol boils) and 100°C. (the boiling point of water). The alcohol vaporized, along with some of the water. This procedure did not yield quite the result he had planned, but instead resulted in the first brandy.

This process of separating alcohol from water is called *distillation*. One of the earliest, simplest methods of distillation involved use of a pot still. The pot still consisted of a central container where a mash (fermented alcohol and water

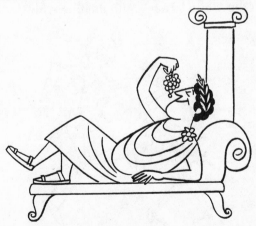

mixture) was heated to a temperature between 78°C. and 100°
C. The alcohol vapors then passed through a coil submerged
in cold water and collected in cooled, liquid form in a bottle at
the end of the coil. The pot still, in a modern, improved form,
is still used in some countries for whiskey and brandy production.

The patent still, a distillation method invented in 1830,
consisted of two columns of horizontal plates. The alcohol-
and-water mixture was poured into the top of the first column
and heated with steam as it dribbled down through the layers.
Alcohol vapors rose out of the first column and passed
through a tube to the second column where it was further
purified and then condensed to a liquid. This method, in a
more complex form, is the basis of some modern distillation
techniques.

With a name like "water of life," alcohol obviously com-
manded respect in many societies. In some cultures, it acquired a holy, magical, or medicinal reputation. People re-
vered—and feared—liquor's ability to cause such damages in
a drinker's mind and body.

Not everybody enjoyed or worshipped the powers of alcohol, though. Religious organizations, most notably those of
the early nineteenth century, initiated a temperance movement in many countries. The movement gained great momentum in the United States, culminating with the National

Prohibition Amendment of 1920 to 1933. Many Americans who lived through Prohibition remember the terrible taste of bootleg gin. Prohibition failed to completely stop the manufacture, sale, and transportation of alcoholic beverages (as Congress intended), but instead forced many people to drink vile-tasting, illegally produced liquor for thirteen years.

After Prohibition, Americans all but forgot the stigma once attached to liquor. As more and more people began drinking alcoholic beverages, they learned new ways to mix, stir, shake, and blend their favorite drinks. The vast and varied history of alcohol has contributed a great deal to the plight of the modern Problem Drinkmaker—bartenders now have thousands of traditional recipes to choose from, with hundreds arriving on the scene each year. Who knows—maybe *you'll* invent a smash new drink someday and change the course of alcohol's future. But first, learn the basics . . .

Whiskies

Whiskey, whisky, Scotch, Irish, Canadian, bourbon, rye, blended, straight . . . confused? They are *all* whiskies, but they differ by country of origin, primary base grain, or variations in processing.

A novice bartender may have some trouble understanding the differences among whiskies. Once you learn a few basics, however, it won't be too difficult to tell them all apart. You'll find that it helps to learn which brand-name whiskies in your bar are of similar origin and quality so you'll know which ones can be interchanged when necessary.

Whiskey production involves four steps: malting, fermenting, distilling, and aging. That last step imparts color to the whiskey; colorless alcohol goes into wooden barrels to age, and interaction between the wood and the liquor supplies flavor, aroma, and color to the whiskey. As soon as whiskey is bottled, the aging stops.

Whiskey or whisky? Which spelling is correct? If you look at a bottle of Four Roses (American), for example, you will see the word *whiskey*. Now read one of your Chivas Regal (Scotch) bottles: *whisky*. As a rule, Scotch and Canadian distillers spell the word without the *e*, and American and Irish whiskey producers include it.

Before trying to serve whiskey, you should understand the difference between *straight* and *blended*. Some blended whiskies contain mixtures of similar products made by different distillers at different times (as in Scotch); others have combinations of straight whiskies and neutral, flavorless whiskies (as in Canadian). Straight whiskies, on the other hand, are not mixed at all, or are mixed only with whiskey from the same distillation period or distiller.

A very important difference among whiskies concerns its country of origin. Scotch, Irish, Canadian and American whiskies are all made by different processes and, therefore, have very distinctive tastes.

Scotch, the whisky of Scotland, usually has barley (and sometimes corn) as its primary base grain. Scotch tastes smoky, a flavor which it acquires when the barley malt roasts over open peat fires during the first step in production. Then this smoky-flavored malt is combined with water (the mash), fermented, distilled in a pot still, and aged at least three years in uncharred oak barrels or used sherry casks. All Scotches imported to the United States have been aged at least four years; the best ones are twelve years old. Most contain blends of whiskies and have been bottled at 80 to 86 proof.

Irish whiskey, a product of Eire and Northern Ireland, uses

barley and other grains as its primary bases. Its ingredients and the methods used to make it are similar to those of Scotch. During Irish whiskey production, however, the malt roasts over coal-fired kilns, so Irish whiskey does not have Scotch's smoky flavor. Sometimes the Irish blend their whiskies for a lighter product. It is then aged 5 to 10 years in used sherry casks and bottled at 86 proof.

Canadian whiskies may contain corn, rye, wheat, and barley as primary base grains. They are always blends of flavored and neutral whiskies which are aged at least four years and bottled at 80 to 86 proof.

American whiskies include bourbon, rye, corn, bottled-in-bond, sour mash, and blended.

Bourbon, named for Bourbon County, Kentucky, where this whiskey originates, is distilled from a fermented mash of at least 51 percent corn. The balance of the mash may contain any other grain, usually rye and barley. The aging process takes 2 to 12 years in oak barrels, after which the bourbon is bottled at 80 to 90 proof.

Rye whiskey contains at least 51 percent rye grain in its mash. Real rye whiskey (such as Old Overholt) is not as popular as it once was, though, so it usually stays on the back bar. Be alert to this when people order "rye and ginger," for example; they probably want *blended whiskey* (such as Seagram's 7 or VO) and ginger. Odd as it may seem, a person who wants to drink real rye usually has to say just that: "I want rye—I mean *real* rye, not blended whiskey."

Corn whiskey is distilled from a fermented mash of grain containing at least 80 percent corn. Notice the difference between bourbon (51 percent corn) and corn whiskey (80 percent).

In the United States, bottled-in-bond whiskey is straight whiskey which was bottled at 100 proof and aged at least four years in United States government-bonded warehouses.

Sour mashes contain some proportion of previously fermented yeast (as opposed to sweet mash, which is made only from fresh yeast). Jack Daniel's Tennessee Whiskey is made from a sour mash.

The difference between straight and blended American whiskies may seem confusing at first. Straight means the mash must contain at least 51 percent of a certain grain:

Mash	*Whiskey*
51% barley	straight malt whiskey
51% rye	straight rye whiskey
51% corn	straight bourbon whiskey
80% corn	straight corn whiskey

Blended whiskies are made from combinations of similar straight whiskies from different distillations or distillers.

Choosing the right whiskey (or whisky) depends on your preferences. At a party, most hosts will provide at least two whiskies: Scotch and bourbon (and usually also a blended selection). Professional bars stock a variety of whiskies, so there you'll have a better chance of finding your favorite type and brand.

Taste-test different brands and read price tags to find *your* best whiskey value. Every brand whiskey varies in flavor according to its base grains, production techniques, and aging, so it is impossible to generalize about which is best. More expensive brands have probably been made with high quality grains, careful production regulations (for a consistently good whiskey), and longer aging periods. On the other hand, some expensive brands owe their premium price tags in part to having been heavily advertised so that people will pay for their image. Bars, of course, also charge more for these prestige brands.

Gin

Deriving its name from the French *genièvre*, meaning "juniper berry," gin was originally prescribed as a diuretic. Although it has no officially sanctioned medicinal value today, many people swear that a couple of martinis can cure a wide variety of ailments.

Gin production involves several steps. First, grains (often corn and rye) are distilled into neutral spirits in a patent still. This grain alcohol is then flavored with juniper berries and other botanicals, distilled again, and bottled at 80 to 100 proof.

Gin brands may vary due to the quality of raw ingredients, the purity of added water, and the recipe of flavorings added prior to the second distillation. Choose your favorite brand by taste-testing different kinds. If you plan to add mixers, subtle brand variations won't matter much, so buy a cheaper brand.

After you buy gin, keep the cap on the bottle or it may spoil. After seven to ten days without a cover, gin may taste slightly milky; if it does, throw it away.

Vodka

According to the Vodka Information Bureau, historians generally credit Poland with the invention of vodka, perhaps as early as the tenth century A.D. Russians quickly adopted this new spirit and gave it its name: *zhizennia voda,* meaning "water of life." They eventually shortened the word to its affectionate diminutive, *vodka,* which translates literally as "dear little water."

Production of dear little water involves three basic steps. First, fermented carbohydrates (usually grain) are distilled to at least 190 proof (dear *big* water) in a patent still. The grain neutral spirits are then diluted, or "cut," with distilled water to 80 to 100 proof, and then filtered through charcoal to remove all distinctive character, aroma, and taste.

All vodkas are created neutral . . . but some are more neutral than others. Hmm . . . Maybe. Many drinkers insist that they can tell the difference between vodkas and can distinguish higher-quality, "more neutral" brands from lower-quality (and lower-priced) "impure" products. They say brands may vary due to the quality of raw materials, the purity of the distilled water added, and the extent of neutrality achieved by the charcoal filtration. If you agree with this and plan to serve your vodka with few or no additional ingredients (a vodka martini, for example), or if you wish to make a good impression on somebody, buy a higher-quality brand. If you plan to combine the vodka with mixers, buy a cheaper brand; vodka should be neutral enough that the mixer can hide the slight imperfections of the cheaper product.

On the other hand, some drinkers insist that a variation in neutrality is impossible or the product is not vodka. It must be devoid of distinctive character, aroma, and taste; therefore—so the argument goes—you could spend varying amounts of money and still end up with vodkas of equal quality. You'll have to judge this debate on your own and choose sides based on your own experimentation.

Rum

Rum production involves the same basic steps used in making many other liquors: Sugar cane juice and molasses (the carbohydrates) are fermented, distilled, sometimes aged, often blended, and then bottled at 80 to 151 proof. Due to variations in this process, you could perhaps find as many kinds of rum as there are brands, but most differ primarily by country of origin.

Puerto Rican rums (such as Bacardi), the most common in America, are light-bodied and dry (not sweet). They are fermented with a special, cultured yeast, then distilled in modern patent stills to over 160 proof (fairly neutral), aged at least one year, and blended with other aged rums. Some Puerto Rican rums have an amber or dark color due to aging in charred oak barrels rather than the plain oak casks used for light rum.

Virgin Islands rum (Ron Virgin, for example) tastes similar to Puerto Rican rum, but is slightly heavier and usually not aged.

Barbados rum (such as Mount Gay) also tastes heavier than Puerto Rican rum and has a darker color. Alexis Lichine, editor of the *Encyclopedia of Wines and Spirits*, describes Barbados rum as characterized by a soft, rather smoky flavor.

Jamaican rum (such as Myers's) is the darkest, richest variety. Whereas Puerto Rican production uses a cultured yeast, molasses for Jamaican rum is fermented naturally. Then it is distilled to less than 160 proof (which leaves some of the molasses flavor in the liquor), aged, often colored with caramel to darken the final product, and bottled at 80 to 100 proof.

You might also come across rums from other regions in your bartending career, such as Haiti (Rhum Barbancourt), New England (Caldwell's Newburyport), Martinique, and Java, but these types are not as common.

Two other Puerto Rican rums merit special recognition so you will know how to mix them into drinks. Some specialty drinks (Zombies, for example) call for 151-proof rum as an ingredient. Do *not* substitute 151-proof rum for regular bar rum (usually around 80 proof); it contains almost twice as much alcohol. Spiced Puerto Rican rum (Captain Morgan's, for example), on the other hand, can be used as a substitute for regular rum as requested by the drinker. It contains the same amount of alcohol, but with the addition of vanilla and other spices which impart more zest to the drink.

Tequila

Poor tequila. Nobody understands it. Even some bar books still treat tequila as a mysterious Mexican potion full of worms, germs, and hallucinogens.

Actually, tequila producers must adhere to strict government quality controls which pretty much take all the mystery—and certainly all the germs—out of the liquor. According to Marion Gorman and Felipe P. de Alba, authors of *The Tequila Book*, tequila must be made from blue agave plants (*Tequilana weber*, blue variety) grown in a specific, government-designated area of Mexico (which includes the town of Tequila). It must go through two distillations and contain at least 51 percent fermented agave juice.

Notice how production of tequila involves basically the same steps as other distilled spirits: A mixture of at least 51 percent blue agave juice and up to 49 percent sugar cane juice (the carbohydrate) is fermented, distilled twice in pot stills, filtered through charcoal, and then either bottled or aged for 1 to 7

years. Aged tequila, called *añejo*, may be stored in used oak barrels, which gives it a golden color. Tequila is 80 proof in the United States, 96 proof in Mexico.

But what about the worm? You'll find worms only in mezcal,

not tequila. Mezcal is another Mexican liquor, similar to tequila, but it is not subject to the same quality controls; mezcal may contain other varieties of the agave from *any* area of Mexico. Gorman and de Alba assure readers that the mezcal worm is harmless and clean. Originally, distillers probably put it there because the worm spends its entire life cycle in the agave plant, so burying it in mezcal seemed the natural thing to do. Today, the worm in a mezcal bottle represents tradition—or merely a sales gimmick.

Brandy

Brandy is distilled from wine or from a fermented fruit mash. If it is made from wine (i.e., from grapes), the term brandy stands alone, but if distilled from another fruit, brandy is called by the fruit name. For example, apricot brandy contains an apricot base. Some brandies, however, have special names:

- Cognac, usually considered the finest of brandies, comes from the Cognac region of France.
- Armagnac, another fine brandy, comes from the Gers region of France.
- Metaxa is a sweet, dark, grape-based Greek brandy.
- Ouzo, another Greek product, is colorless and tastes like licorice.
- Calvados, an apple brandy from the Calvados region of France, is similar to applejack, an American apple brandy.
- Kirschwasser, or kirsch, is a clear cherry brandy of European origin.

Liqueurs

Liqueurs (or cordials) were originally invented as aphrodisiacs! Today's liqueurs contain various plants, fruits, and other flavorings, and are often very colorful. All contain at least 2½ percent sugar, but most have much more than that. In fact, the prefix *crème de,* as in crème de menthe and crème de cacao, refers to the high sugar content of the liqueurs, which gives them a creamy consistency.

Liqueurs of the same flavor base generally stand together on the back bar. To help you learn which ones taste similar, and can therefore be interchanged when necessary, the following list offers a partial grouping of common liqueurs according to flavor.

Almond: amaretto, crème de noyaux, and crème de almond.

Amaretto di Saronno is a high quality, rather expensive amber-colored liqueur, delicious on its own, in mixed drinks, and in coffee. You may substitute other brands to save money in some drinks, but choose carefully because many do not taste the same as the original.

Crème de almond and crème de noyaux are quite similar; you can interchange these red liqueurs in mixed drinks if necessary.

Anise: See Licorice and anise, page 146.

Black Currants: crème de cassis (used for kir).

Black Raspberry: Chambord.

Caraway: Kummel, akvavit.

Cherry: maraschino.

Cocoa: crème de cacao.

Crème de cacao comes in both brown and white (clear). Both colors taste the same, but lend very different appearances to the final drink, so be careful choosing which color to mix.

Coconut and rum: Cocoribe, Malibu.

Coffee: Kahlúa, Tia Maria, coffee brandy.

You can sometimes interchange these and other similar products in mixed drinks, either to save money or when you've run out of something. People often order Kahlúa by name, though; if they don't (in a drink such as a sombrero), use coffee brandy instead to save money. Tia Maria contains Jamaican rum with coffee flavoring; a customer may accept it instead of Kahlúa in a pinch.

Cranberry: Boggs, Cranberria.

Cream: Bailey's Irish Cream, Myers's Rum Cream, Belle Bonne, Venetian Cream, toasted almond cream, McGuire's Original Cream, and so on.

Sweet cream liqueurs contain cream, alcohol, and flavorings. The alcohol preserves the cream so the liqueur can be stored and served at any temperature. In a sense, these liqueurs are premixed cream cocktails, so usually contain relatively little alcohol.

Hazelnut: Frangelico.

Herbs and Spices: Benedictine D.O.M., B and B (brandy and Benedictine), Campari, Chartreuse, Pimm's No.1, Pisang Ambon, and others.

Benedictine and Chartreuse both date from the sixteenth century and contain secret blends of many herbs and spices. Chartreuse comes in both yellow and green (very light colors) and Benedictine is amber-colored.

Campari is a bitter, amber, Italian liqueur.

Pimm's No.1 contains herbs, spices, and various fruits in its blend.

Pisang Ambon is a green, bitter, orange-and-spice-flavored Dutch liqueur.

Licorice and anise: absinthe, anisette, Galliano, ouzo (actually a brandy), Pernod, sambuca.

Absinthe, which contains a dangerous, narcotic ingredient (wormwood), is illegal in the United States, so use Pernod as a substitute.

Galliano, a golden vanilla-licorice liqueur, comes in a very tall bottle and goes into drinks containing the word *golden*, such as Golden Dream and Golden Cadillac.

Melon: Midori.

Many other melon liqueurs have appeared on the market recently in the wake of Midori's success. Taste them before trying to substitute to make sure they taste the same as Midori; many aren't as good, but some will blend nicely into mixed drinks.

Mint: crème de menthe, peppermint schnapps.

Crème de menthe comes in two colors: green and white (clear). Many people drink it as an after-dinner cordial, or between courses of a meal to clean the palate. Consider color in deciding which crème de menthe to put into a mixed drink. Most recipes will tell you which one to use.

Schnapps, a clear, light-bodied crème de menthe, is popular on the rocks, as a shot, and in some mixed drinks.

Orange: Grand Marnier, Cointreau, triple sec, curaçao.

Cointreau (clear, bittersweet) and Grand Marnier (orange-colored, cognac-based) are brand name orange liqueurs.

Curaçao comes in both orange and a pretty blue. Make sure you use orange when no color is specified, and blue when the recipe says blue curaçao.

Triple sec, a clear, tart liqueur, is not as sweet as curaçao. When a recipe calls for Cointreau and you don't have it or you're trying to save money, substitute triple sec.

Sloe berry: sloe gin.

Sloe gin, neither slow nor gin, obtains its flavor from sloe berries, the fruit of the blackthorn bush. This red liqueur is popular in sloe gin fizzes and Sloe Screws.

Violet: crème de violette, Crème Yvette, Parfait Amour.

These liqueurs are violet-flavored and -colored.

Whiskey: Drambuie, Irish Mist, Southern Comfort, Rock and Rye, and others.

Whiskey and honey combine in two popular liqueurs: Drambuie, which is Scotch-based, and Irish Mist, made of Irish whiskey.

Southern Comfort is a bourbon-based, sweet tasting, 100-proof liqueur flavored with peaches and other ingredients. Drinks with the word *comfortable* or *comfort* in their names contain Southern Comfort.

Rock and Rye is rye whiskey flavored with fruit and rock candy.

Yogurt and Cognac: Trenais.

Many liqueurs contain the name of the fruit in the name of the product. For example, the names crème de banana and strawberry liqueur should make it easy for even a chronic Problem Drinkmaker to figure out the main ingredient.

This list is perforce incomplete. Anyone who reads newspapers, magazines, and billboards knows that new liqueurs are being introduced even as you read these words, so a good bartender must stay on top of current trends and new products.

Liquor Quality Classification

Even as a Problem Drinkmaker, you probably had *some* concept of brand classification. You might have heard one friend ooh and aah over a gift of Haig & Haig Pinch Scotch, or another refuse to drink anything but Tanqueray. Maybe you noticed some advertisements had a certain air about them—one of class and prestige. On the other end of the spectrum, perhaps you felt just a bit ill after imbibing that generic swill you bought for one dollar a gallon.

The accepted way to designate liquor quality in bartending is by the "shelf." High-quality, prestige brands are "top shelf"; good, less expensive brands are "middle shelf"; and cheaper brands or generic liquors are classified as "bottom shelf" or "speed rack."

In most bars, customers pay more for "call" brands—those top- and middle-shelf brands that they ask for by name. Managers have devised systems to let the bartender know how much to charge; whether it be a colored dot on the bottle, a list by the cash register, or just a general rule that certain shelves on the bar cost more.

For your home bar, buy your favorite brands. If you have absolutely no idea how to distinguish Boodles from Bob's Booze or Dewar's from dishwater, ask friends for advice, talk to the liquor store clerk, and read magazine and newspaper columns. Start off with middle-shelf brands so you won't strain your budget with high-priced liquors you can't fully appreciate.

Beer

No doubt, beer has been around for a long time. That chewed-up grain brew discussed on page 132 was probably the first primitive beer. Although you won't find today's brewers sitting around the beer plant chewing barley, modern production still involves natural products brewed in a traditional way.

As a beertender or even just a beer drinker, you will come in contact with hundreds of brands and several different types of brew. Yet, despite the popularity of this beverage, very few people (even non–Problem Drinkmakers) know much about it.

The best way to understand the differences among beers is to learn how it's made. The following steps describe a basic beer brewing process.

1. ***Malt preparation:*** The brewer steeps barley (other carbohydrates may be used, but barley is most common) in water and heats it to begin the beer-making process. This step imparts color and taste to the beer; depending on the degree of roasting, the final product will be either pale and light or dark and robust.
2. ***Mashing:*** Mashing involves a rather complicated process for preparing the malted barley. The malt

enzymes break down the starch to sugar and the complex proteins of the malt to simpler nitrogen compounds.

3. *Lautering:* The brewer removes spent grains and continues brewing the liquid.

4. *Boiling and hopping:* The liquid is poured into huge kettles and boiled for about two hours, during which time hops are added to the brew. Hops, the dried flower cones of the hop vine, give beer a sharp, bitter flavor, which is a nice balance to the sweetness of malt sugars. Hops also contribute a pleasant aroma to the brew and help preserve freshness. This unfermented mixture of barley, malt, and hops is called the wort.

5. *Hop separation and cooling:* After the wort has taken the flavor of the hops, they are removed and the brew passes through a cooling device.

6. *Fermentation:* The wort is transferred to fermenting vessels, and yeast is added. The yeast, which are living, single-celled fungi, take the sugar in the brew and break it down to carbon dioxide and alcohol. The brewer can use two species of yeast and, depending on which he chooses, produce ale or lager.

7. *Storage:* After fermentation, the beer is cooled and placed in storage for at least two to four weeks.

8. *Packaging:* The beer is bottled and passes through a pasteurizer where the temperature of the beer is raised to 140°F. to kill the yeast, then cooled to room temperature. The bottles are then capped and sold.

The word "beer" generally covers both ale and lager, although many people use it specifically as a synonym for lager. Both products undergo basically the same brewing process, but a few variations account for the distinctly different tastes of the two.

Very few people order a "lager" at a bar; most ask for a "beer," or perhaps a "Bud" or a "Becks dark." Lager is brewed at relatively low temperatures (around 55°C.) using a "bottom-fermenting" yeast, meaning a yeast that works mostly from the bottom of the barrel. The brewer then draws the lager off the top, leaving the yeast in the tank.

By contrast, ale is brewed at higher temperatures (around 60°C.) using a "top-fermenting" yeast—a yeast that floats on top of the brew during fermentation and then must be skimmed off. Ale tastes hoppier (more bitter) than lager and has a higher alcohol content (4.4 to 5.5 percent, as opposed to lager's 3.2 to 4.5 percent). Popular ales include Molson Golden, Ballantine, and Bass.

Pilsner beer (such as Pilsner Urquell) is a kind of lager beer named for the famous brews of Pilsen, Czechoslovakia. As a bartender, you will serve a lot of "light" Pilsners (Miller Lite, Amstel Light), which were brewed with extra enzymes and therefore have lower calorie, carbohydrate, and alcohol contents. Light beers contain 68 to 134 calories per 12 ounces (other beers have 150 to 180 calories) and 2.5 to 3.2 percent alcohol.

Porter and stout are sweet, dark-brown ales. Stout (such as Guinness) tastes slightly hoppier than porter (Narragansett, Anchor), has a thicker texture, and contains 5 to 6 percent alcohol.

Malt liquor (Colt 45, Schlitz Malt Liquor) is a lager that has a higher alcohol content than other lagers (over 5 percent). It tastes hoppier than beer, yet lighter than ale.

Bock beer (such as Genesee Bock) is a sweet, heavy, amber-to-dark-colored lager beer containing 3.5 percent alcohol.

To help you keep track of all these different beers, here's a quick summary.

Lagers	*Ales*
Light-colored lager	Pale Ale
Dark lager	Brown Ale
Pilsner	Porter
Light beer	Stout
Malt liquor	
Bock	

Now that you're an expert on beer-brewing techniques and can distinguish your ales from your elbow, make sure you handle this precious substance with kid gloves. Precious? Kid gloves? Beer?? Believe it or not, beer is a sensitive liquid and must be handled carefully. Though the word *lager* comes from a German word meaning "to store" or "to keep," that's the last thing you should do to packaged beer. Beer improves over time in the brewing process, but bottled beer has a peak life expectancy of only six months, canned beer only half that time, and kegs (which are unpasteurized) only one month. Keep this in mind when you see amazing beer sales. For instance, a huge sign in a liquor store proclaiming BEER— ONLY 50¢ A CASE! could indicate one of three things: (a) the store owner is a terrific guy; (b) the store owner is a terrible businessman; or (c) the beer is old.

Beer is sensitive to temperature extremes and to light, so store it in a cool, dark area (such as the bottom of your refrigerator). The ideal temperature is somewhere between 40°F. and 60°F. At higher temperatures, the ingredients break down and the aroma and flavor deteriorate, resulting in "skunked" beer. When frozen, the solids separate from the liquid and form flakes which do not go back into solution when the beer thaws.

Keg beer (also called "draft" or "tap") demands extra-special attention. It is not pasteurized and must be refrigerated at all times. (For more information about kegs, see chapter 4, pages 103-4.)

Several brewers have come out recently with "beer balls"

as a smaller alternative to the keg. These 5 ⅙-gallon, spherical, plastic minikegs may be more convenient than bottles or cans in states with returnable bottle laws.

To serve the perfect beer, start with a sparkling clean beer glass dipped in cold water. You should keep special glasses just for beer; a film on the glass—from milk or detergent, for example—can alter the taste of the beer. Also, when washing the glasses, never wipe them with a towel or place them on a towel to dry. Instead, allow them to dry on a corrugated drainboard or a rack so air can circulate freely inside and out.

For a thick, foamy head, pour the beer straight down the middle of the glass from about one inch above the rim. For a smaller head, tilt the glass and pour down the side; then, before it is completely filled, bring it upright.

Then, bottoms up!

Wine

"Everything you always wanted to know about wine in several easy pages." Ridiculous? You bet it is. Therefore, on the following few pages, you will not learn everything you always wanted to know about wine, but only what you need to know to get started as a bartender. If you're still curious, buy a wine book, read wine columns in magazines and newspapers, or enroll in a wine appreciation course. The result of this research will be well worth the effort. As Shakespeare noted, "Good wine is a good familiar creature if it be well used" (*Othello*, Act II, scene 3, line 315).

According to Toni, the Harvard Bartending Course's wine consultant, the best way to learn about wines is to *taste* them. Reading tells you what the experts like and what they look for in a wine, but you should try different kinds to find *your* favorites.

To find a good wine at a reasonable price, look for sales and ask the wine store clerk for advice. Exchange rates cause imported wine prices to fluctuate, so sometimes you can find a very good import at a nice price.

Currently, white wine outsells red and rosé by about 5 to 1, although recent trends suggest this may shift in the future. If you are watching your budget and, therefore, can afford only a limited selection for your bar, buy a popular dry to medium white wine (not sweet). With more money, splurge on a rosé or red, but you don't really have to, since white wine is so popular. For more budget-minded wine hints, see page 104.

Wines are variously classified according to color, type, place of origin, grape variety, and vintage year. Understanding these categories will help you select and serve wines with confidence and some degree of expertise.

Even Problem Wine-appreciators can distinguish white wine from rosé from red just by looking at them, but not all of them know that wine color does *not* indicate what color grapes they contain, or that many white wines come from red grapes. The fact is that wine color depends on how long the grape skins stayed in the wine during fermentation; skins remain in white wine for a short time, and red wine for a longer period.

Some other myth-busters are:

Myth: Chablis is another name for white wine.
Fact: Chablis originated in a specific area of France. Although American winemakers now produce a Chablis similar to the original, the term still refers to a specific kind of dry wine. Many white wines are not Chablis. This misunderstanding arose because many bars and restaurants serve some kind of Chablis as the house

wine, so customers now use the term generically to refer to all white wines.

Myth: Burgundy is another name for red wine.
Fact: As with the "Chablis syndrome," red wines are not all Burgundy—and not all Burgundys are red.

Myth: Rosé contains a blend of red and white wines.
Fact: Rosé is the product of a shortened version of the process used to make red wine; the grape skins are removed sooner (though not so promptly that white wine results).

A small sip will tell you if you're drinking still, sparkling, or fortified wine. Still wines—red, white, and rosé—are noncarbonated beverages containing 7 to 15 percent alcohol. Sparkling wines, such as champagne, sparkling Burgundy, and Asti Spumanti, may also be red, white, or rosé, with 7 to 15 percent alcohol, but they are *all* bubbly. Fortified wines, such as port and sherry, contain brandy, which brings the alcohol content up to 18 to 22 percent. Dubonnet and vermouth have other flavorings added as well as brandy and are called "aromatics."

With wines from California, if the wine contains at least 51 percent of a certain grape, it is referred to by that grape name. Some common "varietal" wines include, from driest to sweetest: chardonnay, fumé blanc, chenin blanc, riesling, and sauterne.

Just read the wine label to find out where and when the product was made. Most wines in America come from France, Italy, Germany, Spain, Portugal, Japan, and America. (Japanese wine, called sake, is made from fermented rice instead of grapes.) If the wine was made from grapes harvested in a certain year, this vintage date appears on the label.

In storage, keep wine bottles on their sides so the corks will stay moist, and protect them from temperature extremes and light. As a general rule, serve red wine at room temperature and white wine chilled.

Does everything make more sense now? Knowing how liquor, beer, and wine are made should help you understand why certain flavor combinations work best and why some brands taste better than others. With this dangerously small amount of knowledge, you can even invent your own drinks.

:6:

Side Effects

Advertisers say it's sexy, glamorous, fun, exciting, relaxing, rewarding, and magical. It's hard to imagine that this marvelous elixir, alcohol, could have side effects, isn't it? Well, just like plenty of other wonderful things in life, *too much* alcohol can make you:

- lose control of your motor skills
- gain weight
- act like a fool
- become sick
- experience distorted vision
- lose consciousness
- spend time in jail
- pay hefty fines
- become addicted
- die

Of course, this is just a partial list to catch your attention. That last little item startled you a bit? About 25,000 people will suffer from that side effect this year when they try to drink and drive. Many more will die as a result of other alcohol-related illnesses.

If you plan to pour, mix, or drink liquor, you need to know about these side effects so you can protect yourself and the people you serve. This chapter will help you understand alcohol better by explaining:

The physiology of alcohol: How the body metabolizes alcohol. What process makes a person become
drunk. How much an individual can drink before
being considered drunk.
Hangovers: The causes of hangovers. Is there a
cure?
Other side effects: Liquor's effect on other parts of
the body besides the brain. Why alcohol can be
fattening.
Serious side effects: Alcohol abuse and the problem
drinker. Drinking and driving.
Bartenders' responsibilities: Legal issues.

Up to now, you've been encouraged to relax, just skim
through the pages, and enjoy yourself. Please try to read this
chapter more carefully, though. Well, okay, you *can* skim the
parts on the hangover and the fattening effects of alcohol—
you'll probably learn those subjects through experience anyway. Read the last sections, from "Alcohol Abuse" to the end
of the chapter, especially attentively. Bartenders must become more involved in helping to control these problems if
we ever hope to see such issues dealt with effectively.

Physiology

Did you know that the body is actually a natural distillery?
Through a fermentation process, it transforms food sugars into
about one ounce of ethanol each day. When it takes in additional
alcohol, however, the excess is absorbed into the bloodstream
and affects various parts of the body until the alcohol eventually
oxidizes.

The liquor you drink contains ethyl alcohol. The primary
distinction between ethyl and other alcohols is that ethanol
metabolizes rapidly into relatively harmless substances, whereas
the other alcohols metabolize slowly into poisons. Remember

those old comedy routines in which the drunk stole rubbing alcohol from the detoxification hospital to satisfy his craving? Rubbing alcohol contains isopropyl alcohol, not ethanol, so the poor guy probably suffered from much more than a hangover. In fact, even a small amount of isopropyl alcohol can cause permanent blindness—no laughing matter.

Three basic steps take place when the body processes alcohol: absorption, distribution, and oxidation. In the absorption phase, unlike most foods, alcohol passes rapidly into the bloodstream without being digested. Some is absorbed rather slowly through the mouth and some through the stomach lining, but most goes into the small intestine. From there, it is absorbed quickly into the bloodstream.

Certain variables alter this process. Have you ever noticed you get drunk faster on an empty stomach? Food keeps alcohol in the stomach longer (where absorption takes place slowly) and delays its passage to the small intestine (where abosrption takes place rapidly). Bear in mind, however, that the alcohol will eventually make it to the small intestine, so gorging yourself will only delay the effects.

Does champagne make you feel tipsy faster than wine? Bubbles make you get drunker faster. The carbon dioxide in any carbonated drink hastens the movement of alcohol through the stomach to the small intestine and into the bloodstream.

Body weight is also a major consideration in the attempt to gauge alcohol's effect on the drinker. Size has a great deal of influence on how drunk a person gets—larger people have more "substance" throughout which to dilute the alcohol. For instance, a ninety-pound weakling might be very obviously affected by just one drink, while, in the same period of time, a heavyweight could consume three without much of a reaction.

Once the alcohol enters the bloodstream, it passes to body organs in proportion to the amount of water they contain. The brain, with its high concentration of water, retains a great deal of alcohol, and the effects become apparent very quickly. Therefore, the most immediate and noticeable characteristics of drunkenness occur as a result of alcohol's "attack" on the brain.

The most pronounced brain responses vary directly with the amount of alcohol measured in the bloodstream. For that reason, a fairly good indication of what the brain is up against is a measurement called the blood alcohol concentration (BAC), the percentage of alcohol in the bloodstream. (Sometimes this measurement is referred to as the BAL, blood alcohol level.) Alcohol is a depressant drug, so when the BAC rises, more areas of the brain become depressed.

Reactions to alcohol vary tremendously among individuals, but when the BAC reaches .05 percent in the *average* person, the outer layer of the brain becomes drugged and sluggish. This outer layer controls inhibitions, self-restraint, and judgement— or at least it *did* when it was sober. When alcohol numbs this control center, most inhibitions fly out the window, and drinkers usually find they have a lot more to say about everything. With this new-found sociability and vivaciousness, people often forget that alcohol is a depressant. They think that because drinking causes them to lose their inhibitions, it must therefore

be a stimulant. Remember, though, that this feeling stems from the *depression* of a brain part, not the stimulation of it.

At a BAC of .10 percent, the motor area of the brain (anterior) becomes depressed. You'll feel pretty depressed yourself if you're caught drinking and driving at this BAC level—most states consider it the minimum level of legal intoxication. At .10 percent BAC, coordination becomes quite impaired. The drinker staggers, slurs words, and can't quite fit the key in the keyhole. By this point, just about all inhibitions have been drowned.

At .20 percent BAC, alcohol affects the midbrain, the section which controls emotional behavior. A drinker at this stage acts— as they say—smashed. Sensory and motor skills have deteriorated to the point where many drinkers need to lie down. Some laugh, some cry, some become angry, some feel romantic . . . and some try to feel all these emotions at the same time.

A .30 percent BAC depresses the lower portion of the brain, which controls sensory perception. At this level, drinkers virtually lose consciousness; although awake, they have very little comprehension of the world around them. As the saying goes, "The lights are on, but nobody's home." It's amazing, though, how many people can make absolute fools of themselves when they can barely see or hear. Fortunately, many drinkers "black out" (forget) these embarrassing escapades; the pain of the hangover would be excruciating if aggravated by such humiliating memories.

Between .35 and .45 percent BAC, the party's over. A drinker at this level enters a coma and should be brought to a hospital. A BAC of .35 percent is generally the minimum level which causes death, but often the coma is the body's defense mechanism *against* death. In this state, a patient will not drink anymore, so the body stands a better chance of keeping its BAC down to a level of survival.

At .60 percent BAC, the part of the brain which controls those little everyday activities like breathing and heartbeat becomes depressed. Some young fools reach this level by accepting a ten-dollar dare to chug a fifth of liquor. A quick fifth will blast through all the stages discussed up to this point and kill the drinker in minutes. Some drinkers who try to reach this point but move too slowly will end up in a mere coma.

The Brain Drain Chart

This chart summarizes the effects of the blood alcohol concentration (BAC) on the brain of an average person. These responses vary, however, from person to person, and from day to day. Another chart on page 164 approximates the number of drinks it takes to reach these levels.

BAC (%)	Effects
.05	Release of inhibitions and self-restraint; poor judgement
.10	Loss of coordination: staggering, slurring, clumsiness; impaired vision
.20	Dulled sensory perception; loss of emotional control
.30	Virtual loss of consciousness; blackout
.35–.40	Coma; minimum lethal level
.60	Death

Although alcohol moves quickly into the body and takes rapid effect, getting it out of circulation takes a long time.

Sobering up occurs through a process called oxidation in which the liver breaks alcohol down into water and carbon dioxide. For most foods, the rate of oxidation increases with activity. That is, as the body needs more energy, it breaks down the food faster. Alcohol, however, has a constant rate of oxidation which cannot be increased through exercise. For most people, that rate is about one-half ounce of alcohol (about one drink) per hour. What does this mean? That's right—sobering up is just a matter of *time* (or not drinking in the first place). All the walking, black coffee, fresh air, and cold showers in the world will not speed it up.

How much can a person drink before becoming drunk?

You may have seen weight/alcohol consumption charts in magazines, liquor stores, and bars. The charts provide a handy drinking formula so you can figure out approximately how drunk you are after each drink. Do *not* rely on these charts. The only variables they take into consideration are weight, time, number of drinks consumed, and sometimes sex (to account for different metabolisms). In reality, many other factors play an important role in determining degrees of intoxication.

- How much *sleep* did the drinker get last night? A tired person will show the effects of alcohol more readily than an alert drinker.
- Did the drinker take any *medication?* Medicine alters alcohol's effects, sometimes drastically. Be very cautious mixing any two drugs, especially when one of them is alcohol.
- How *old* is the drinker? Younger people usually become drunk on fewer drinks. Older people's vision generally deteriorates more rapidly as the BAC increases.
- Is the drinker's *liver* in good shape? The liver plays a major

role in the sobering process and thus greatly influences the degree of inebriation.

● Is the drinker in a good *mood?* An especially happy, sad, angry, or other mood probably will alter the person's response to alcohol.

● How does the drinker's *metabolism* work? Some people oxidize alcohol faster than others. BAC can vary widely, even when many other factors remain constant.

A faulty assumption people often make is that beer or wine will not get them as drunk as a drink made with higher-proof liquor. Wrong. A cocktail, a beer, a 5-ounce glass of wine, and a 3-ounce glass of sherry all have about the same amount of alcohol in them—.6 ounces.

The following chart will give you some idea of *approximately* how many drinks it takes the average person to reach each BAC.

Relationships Among Sex, Weight, Oral Alcohol Consumption, and Blood Alcohol Level

		Blood Alcohol Levels (mg/100 ml)			
Alcohol (oz.)	Drinks* per hr.	Female 100 lbs	Female 150 lbs	Male 150 lbs	Male 200 lbs
½	1	.045	.03	.025	.019
1	2	.09	.06	.05	.037
2	4	.18	.12	.10	.07
3	6	.27	.18	.15	.11
4	8	.36	.24	.20	.15
5	10	.45	.30	.25	.18

*1 ounce of 100-proof spirits, a 12-oz. beer, 5oz. of wine, or 3 oz. of sherry.

SOURCE: Ray, Oakley: *Drugs, Society and Human Behavior*, 3d ed. (St. Louis; C. V. Mosby Co., 1983). Used by permission.

The Hangover

Seven A.M. The noise of the alarm clock drills through your fuzzy head and pounds mercilessly on your brain. "Uh-oh," you think groggily, as one half-opened, red-rimmed eye squints through the fog at the clock. "I've done it again." Sure enough, with a blinding headache, nausea, stomach pain, and incredible thirst, you're up and off to work. Work? But your mouth and brain won't even cooperate long enough to sound a "Good morning, boss." Good morning, indeed!

If you drink too much, there's a good chance you'll wake up in the morning feeling this lousy. Some say that having drunk champagne intensifies the pain, probably because bubbles deliver the alcohol to the bloodstream so quickly.

Dehydration is what causes a major share of the hangover's pain. Loss of water results in a very thirsty feeling, headache, and overall sluggishness.

The variety of additives and spices added to liquor during production and mixing don't help matters much, either. Your nausea and stomach pains can be attributed in part to a number of flavoring herbs and spices in the liquor itself. Or perhaps the pain intensifies as the result of additives the bartender mixed in. How much orange juice and Tabasco sauce can one stomach stand in a night?

Cures? They say the only real cure for the morning hangover is the afternoon nap. That's fine for some people, but for those who must go to work and keep on living, there must be a better way. Unfortunately there is no real cure except time. There are, however, ways to relieve the pain:

> *Drink plenty of water before bed.* Drink until you're full and then drink some more. Keep a pitcher of water beside your bed in case you wake up during the night so you can drink more. Dehydration is a major cause of hangover pain. All this water will help coun-

teract dehydration, so you'll probably feel much better in the morning.

If you fell asleep before drinking water the night before, *drink plenty the next morning*. Resist the temptation to drink orange juice because the acid in it might make your stomach pains feel worse.

Take a shower, sauna, or steam bath in the morning (not too long in the sauna or steam bath). These "cures" will increase circulation and refresh and open pores so you should feel fresher and more revived.

Take a nonaspirin pain reliever. (Aspirin may upset your queasy stomach, so try to avoid it until you feel better.) A couple of these pain relievers, especially after drinking a lot of water the night before, should reduce headache pain and other general body aches.

If you're really drunk and sure to be hung over in the morning, sometimes the best remedy is—sorry about this—to *empty your stomach*. Vomiting will prevent most of the alcohol left in your stomach from passing into the bloodstream and will rid your stomach of all those irritating additives, spices, and mixers.

What about the "hair of the dog"? Although you'll probably be only postponing the agony, not eliminating it, many people try to "cure" their hangovers with a hair of the dog that bit them. That is, they keep drinking when hangover threatens. Although the alcohol will indeed deaden the brain—and the pain—temporarily, this "cure" is not advisable because it may lead to greater physical problems later.

Another side effect . . . and bottom effect, and front effect: fat

Alcohol oxidation sounds like an all-consuming effort for the body, and indeed it is. Alcohol seems to get a first priority

treatment: it gets rushed through the stomach without digestion, absorbed quickly into the bloodstream, and then oxidized
through a slow, arduous process. Imagine—all that work for
something with no nutritional value!

Meanwhile, back in the stomach, nutritional food just sits
there waiting for the body to get around to oxidizing it. If it waits
too long without being used, it turns instead to fat tissue.

Some alcoholics thought that sounded just fine—they
eliminated the food and lived off the calories in alcohol. This
diet, although possibly a method of weight loss, provides *no*
nutrition to the body. No vitamins, no minerals, nothing.
Besides, when you see how many calories can be packed into
some of your favorite drinks, you just might want to stick to
cottage cheese.

Alcoholic Beverage	Amount	Calories
Beer, ale	12 oz.	about 150
Light beer	12. oz.	about 95
Distilled liquors (whiskey, rum, vodka, gin, etc.)		
80 proof	1½ oz.	97
86 proof	1½ oz.	105
94 proof	1½ oz.	116
Dry table wine	4 oz.	75–100

Mixers	Amount	Calories
Soda water	any	0
Cola	8 oz.	96
Ginger ale	8 oz.	72
Tonic water	8 oz.	72
Sour mix	4 oz.	about 50
Orange juice	8 oz.	100
Cranberry juice	8 oz.	145

If you think *that's* bad . . .

Drink	Amount	Calories
Margarita	12 oz.	375
Piña colada	12 oz.	350
Sangria	12 oz.	250
Frozen daiquiri	12 oz.	300
Strawberry daiquiri	12 oz.	350
Tom Collins	12 oz.	225

These calorie counts may vary depending on the recipe, but you get the idea. If you're watching your weight and would like a drink, try a light beer, a glass of wine, a wine spritzer or cooler, or perhaps the pineapple-wine cooler listed on page 92. If you prefer a distilled spirit, drink it either without mixer, with soda water, or with a low-calorie mixer.

Other short-term effects

The brain isn't the only one to notice alcohol's presence. Even just one drink causes some rather harmless changes in the body; more liquor provokes more serious reactions.

That first drink or two affects the digestive system. It stimulates gastric juices in the stomach and possibly provokes a reaction in the taste buds, both of which serve to increase appetite. For this reason, people often enjoy aperitifs before meals. Aperitifs, alcoholic beverages drunk before the meal to stimulate the appetite, should be rather low in alcohol and not too warm or cold. A glass of wine, a beer, or a cocktail fits this description and serves as a good aperitif.

Too much alcohol might have the opposite effect—it will stop digestion and probably deaden taste buds, thus reducing appetite. On the other hand, some people eat every potato chip in sight whenever they drink too much. This phenomenon can be easily explained—when the inhibitions go, so does the diet.

Raid that refrigerator next time you're drunk! You won't care . . . until the next morning.

When alcohol depresses the brain, the brain, in turn, has trouble handling many other bodily functions. For instance, alcohol throws off the body's water balance, which causes the kidneys to excrete excessive amounts of water. This imbalance explains part of the dehydration problem of hangovers.

An alcohol-drugged brain also results in a lack of motor skills and sensory perception while at the same time promoting a feeling of self-confidence and sociability. This combination of effects presents a number of problems in other areas of the body. As Shakespeare noted in *Macbeth* (Act II, scene 3, line 34), "It [drink] provokes the desire, but it takes away the performance." Decreased sexual performance is only one ego-deflating response of the body to a sluggish brain. Barroom fights pose a similar problem when a macho, overconfident hero has trouble standing up and walking.

These rather minor side effects of alcohol should pose no serious threat to the moderate drinker. In fact, some studies reveal that small quantities of alcohol may even *increase* a person's life span, but the evidence to this effect is inconclusive. At any rate, drinkers probably won't have serious problems unless they get into the habit of periodic binges or of regular heavy drinking.

Alcohol Abuse: The Problem Drinker

Information about alcohol's short-term effects applies only to "social drinkers," people who do not normally have a problem handling liquor, but may occasionally overindulge in certain social situations.

Serious problem drinkers, also called alcoholics when medically diagnosed as such, do not have the control for just an occasional social drink. Sometimes they start out that way, but discover that alcohol relieves tensions, so they turn to drinking as an escape from problems. As the nervous system builds up a tolerance, problem drinkers require increasing amounts of alcohol and become physically addicted. Most become preoccupied with drinking, yet attempt to hide this obsession from friends and family.

You already know of the havoc alcohol can wreak in just one night of drunkenness. Think of years spent in that condition and you can imagine the debilitating effects on an alcoholic's mind and body. Problem drinkers battle many devastating emotional problems. Unable to avoid regular heavy drinking, alcoholics must often wrestle with family and job difficulties related to their intoxication. It's no wonder that suicide rates run so high among alcoholics.

Emotional problems become compounded by the incredible destruction of an alcoholic's body. Physically addicted to liquor, chronic alcoholics often suffer delirium tremens (DTs) when withdrawing from alcohol without proper medical care. DTs involve three to six days of shaking, fever, acute panic, and vivid hallucinations. This experience sometimes frightens the problem drinker away from alcohol for a while but, unfortunately, many eventually return to their previous condition.

After years of addiction, many problem drinkers virtually stop eating, as alcohol replaces the calories food once provided. Liquor contains no nutritional substance, though, so most alcoholics develop serious vitamin and mineral deficiencies as well as diseases which accompany such malnutrition. Beri beri, a condition resulting from vitamin B shortages, often reveals itself in the alcoholic as "Korsakoff's psychosis" or "Wernicke's syndrome," both characterized by gradual memory loss, confusion, and disorientation.

As the liver plays such a major role in alcohol oxidation, it obviously takes quite a beating from alcohol abuse. After just two days of heavy drinking, a person can develop fatty liver as the result of a breakdown in the mechanism which moves fat from the liver into the blood. Very long periods of drinking increase the severity of this condition, or may lead to alcoholic hepatitis, an inflammation of the liver. Some alcoholics' livers become scarred and hardened from abuse. This condition, cirrhosis, ranks as the third leading cause of death among 25- to 65-year-olds in New York City.

Long-term heavy drinking may also lead to destruction within the digestive and circulatory systems. Many alcoholics develop chronic irritation of the stomach lining as the result of alcohol's constant stimulation of gastric fluids. Some contract cancer of the mouth (especially smokers), pharynx, larynx, or esophagus. After a long period of regularly taxing the heart, alcoholism may also give rise to diseases of the heart muscle and an increased risk of high blood pressure.

At present, doctors and psychologists cannot explain what leads people to problem drinking. Some professionals consider alcoholism a disease which the drinker cannot control. Others believe instead that the drinker's personality plays a major role; troubled people with social adaptation problems turn to heavy drinking as a way to cope with pressures. Perhaps society's view of drinking encourages people to overindulge to the point where many become addicted. Some believe biological differences or an inability to learn controlled drinking from one's family contributes to the development of alcoholism. Unfortunately, until further research provides a satisfying explanation, nobody can be sure of the true cause of alcoholism.

Today, most cures revolve around a detoxification program, which supervises an alcoholic's withdrawal, treats DT symptoms, provides medical care for physical ailments, and offers psychological guidance to ease the reformed alcoholic into a life of abstinence. Some programs prescribe disulfiram (Antabuse), a drug which causes nausea and vomiting when a patient tries to drink. Support groups, such as Alcoholics Anonymous, may help an alcoholic stay on the wagon. Most of these "cures" rest on the assumption that an alcoholic *cannot* learn controlled drinking, but must always abstain completely. Sometimes this approach works, but often the patient slips, has one drink, and resumes heavy drinking. Unfortunately, until doctors and psychologists pinpoint the cause of alcoholism, they cannot prescribe a completely effective cure.

Drunk Driving

These days, just about everyone has lost someone to a drunk driving accident. For those few who haven't experienced the loss of a friend yet, TV news reports will show you what you're missing. Cameras zoom into twisted, burnt cars to show the mangled remains of a body. Reporters rush to interview the victim's family and capture their grief while it is still fresh. Usually, the coroner announces the drinker's BAC to the press who then release every detail to their public. Drunk driving accidents make a good story—people often consider them "more tragic" than other auto accidents, for example, because they occur as the *direct* result of a senseless, *preventable* action. Sure, that *is* tragic and senseless—so why do people keep drinking and driving?

Of the approximately 120 million drivers in the United States, an estimated 88 million of them drink at least occasionally. Twenty-three million reportedly drink heavily, sometimes before driving; these heavy drinkers account for the majority of the 25,000 yearly alcohol-related traffic fatalities.

You don't need a heavy drinker involved to cause an accident, though. Even at .05 percent BAC—only one or two drinks for some people—drivers lose inhibitions and feel more relaxed about everything. Someone at this level of intoxication might misjudge the severity of a driving situation; this person might feel too relaxed and happy to recognize a potential accident until it's too late.

As the BAC increases, driver reflexes deteriorate. A .10 percent BAC usually signals a depressed motor area in the brain, which results in slowed reaction times and uncoordinated movements. How could someone drive safely at .10 percent when the reflexes will *not* respond in an emergency? Of course, there's still the problem that the drinker won't even recognize the emergency, let alone respond to it.

At higher levels, coordination and judgment deteriorate even further. The drinker also develops vision problems as alcohol affects the delicate muscle structure of the eye. With such poor powers of judgment, motor control, and eyesight, driving at this point is almost like asking to die.

The following chart reveals how drivers fare at various levels of intoxication. It shows the statistical relationship between BAC levels and automobile accidents..

BAC (%)	Risk of Accident
.05	2–3 times the normal (sober) risk
.08	5–6 times the normal (sober) risk
.10	7–8 times the normal (sober) risk
above .10	20–50 times the normal (sober) risk

Do you remember all those drunk variables—mood, metabolism, age, and so on—listed earlier in the chapter? Taking those into consideration, the figures in this chart reflect the *lowest* probability for an individual. If someone feels tired, takes medication, has a slow metabolism, a weak liver, or maybe just had a rough day, the chances of accident could skyrocket. People's reactions to alcohol vary from day to day, notwithstanding the old excuse "I have high tolerance to alcohol."

The solution? Put away the statistical charts and BAC weight tables—just do *not* drink and drive. Walk. Call a cab. Have a friend drive you home. Go home with a friend. Crawl on your hands and knees, for heaven's sake, but stay away from the driver's seat. Don't be embarrassed. Taking a chance with your own or another person's life is irresponsible and stupid, over and above what the charts, figures, and statistics say.

What if you do drive, take a wide corner or swerve a bit, and get nabbed by the police? The consequences depend on where you are at the time.

In most states, holding a driver's license means that the authorities have your "implied consent" to give you a breathalyzer test and to require that you take it. If you refuse, you face prosecution, usually in the form of license suspension for 90 to 180 days. States without an implied consent law at this writing include Delaware, Maine, Minnesota, Pennsylvania, and Vermont.

The breathalyzer reveals your BAC level. In many states, a

.10 percent BAC constitutes *per se* evidence of driving under the influence of alcohol—that is, *conclusive* evidence you were drunk driving. States with a per se intoxication level of .10 percent include: Alabama, Alaska, Arizona, California, Delaware, District of Columbia, Florida, Illinois, Maine, Michigan, Minnesota, Missouri, Nebraska, New York, North Carolina, Oklahoma, Oregon, Pennsylvania, South Dakota, Utah, Vermont, Washington, West Virginia, Wisconsin.

Only one state has a per se level higher than .10 percent: Iowa with a .13 percent BAC.

Some states have a "presumptive" BAC level instead of (or in addition to) per se laws. A presumptive level is not a conclusive indication of drunk driving, but merely a piece of evidence strongly suggesting the driver operated under the influence. The final decision rests with the court. States with a presumptive BAC level of .10 percent include: Arkansas, Colorado, Connecticut, Georgia, Hawaii, Indiana, Iowa (in addition to the .13 percent per se law), Kansas, Kentucky, Louisiana, Massachusetts, Michigan, Mississippi, Montana, Nevada, New Hampshire, New Jersey, New Mexico, North Dakota, Ohio, Rhode Island, South Carolina, Tennessee, Texas, Virginia.

States with a lower presumptive BAC include: Washington, D.C. (.05 percent, in addition to .10 percent per se), Idaho (greater than .08 percent), Utah (.08 percent in addition to .10 percent per se).

Only Maryland has a higher presumptive BAC, .13 percent.

To confuse you further, some states have also adopted presumptive BAC levels for a charge of driving while impaired (DWI) as opposed to the more common charge of driving under the influence. States with presumptive DWI provisions include the following: Colorado (.05 percent), Maryland (.08 percent), Michigan (.07 percent).

If you're stupid enough to drink and drive, you should find your state in the above lists (some states appear more than once) and follow those legal guidelines. Don't trust these lists for too long, though—the laws are constantly changing, usually in the direction of stricter legislation against drunk driving. Anyway, unless you go to a bar with a breathalyzer, there's *no* sure way to measure your BAC. The safest way to protect yourself is to abstain from drinking before driving.

The Bartender's Responsibilities— Legal Issues

Why does a bartender need to know so much information about drinking and driving? Remember, judgment is the first response to go in a drinker's brain. How can a person with poor judgment possibly know when to stop drinking if the bartender doesn't step in? Therefore, the bartender should try to keep drinkers sober.

Perhaps concern for your customer's safety and welfare isn't enough to make you go through the hassle of "shutting off" a drunk. It's a lot easier to go on serving intoxicated people to keep them quiet. Besides, drunks often tip better.

Would you feel at least a little bit sorry if your laziness caused a drunken customer to die in an accident or cause some other damages? If you answered no to this question, the government and judicial system would like to change your mind. Nationwide, there has been a recent crackdown on drunk driving. On one hand, the crackdown centers on catching and punishing people who drive under the influence of alcohol. Many states have passed stricter laws to deal with these people, including mandatory jail terms in some instances. On the other hand, legislators have recently been coming to the realization that maybe they should go closer to the *root* of the problem: if people don't *get* drunk, they won't *drive* drunk. After a certain point of lost judgment, however, a drinker cannot decide when to stop. Lawmakers would like to help these people by shifting the responsibility of judgment over to the people who serve liquor.

Dram shop legislation stems from this line of thought. Dram shop laws, statutes on the books of many states, make specific provisions to prosecute the servers of drunks. If a person becomes intoxicated and causes some damage, either the drunk or someone adversely affected by the drunk's actions can sue the establishment that served the liquor. This statute has proved quite popular recently. It is not reserved solely for bars, either. Hosts of private parties have been held liable for damage caused by intoxicated guests.

Many states without dram shop statutes have prosecuted servers of drunks through case law. Suits against bar owners and party hosts established precedents of prosecution for similar subsequent cases.

These laws are getting tougher. At present, bartenders remain protected individually while the establishment or property owner bears the burden of prosecution. In many states, the operator's license may be automatically revoked. In the near future, however, don't be surprised if bartenders must defend themselves legally for damages caused or incurred by their patrons. Be prepared.

How can you protect yourself, your patron, and the bar where you work? For starters, read this chapter carefully to learn how to recognize an intoxicated person. Some bars provide those weight alcohol consumption charts to help you decide how much to serve a person, but these aren't very accurate, so be careful. (Remember, your bar or your party may be a guest's third stop that day.) Recently, some bars have purchased breathalyzers to help patrons decide when to stop drinking and/ or call a cab. Since their use remains voluntary, this method has not been too successful, but it's a step in the right direction.

If a person shows signs of intoxication, do *not* serve that person. Then again, some drinkers can go all night without so much as a slur . . . but then they may get behind the wheel and lose control. To prevent such problems, try to keep track of your customers and don't serve anyone too much, regardless of outward appearance. Unfortunately, this is easier said than done, as many drinkers become belligerent in the face of such humiliation. To avoid unpleasant situations, be very discreet; quietly refuse to serve alcohol, then offer the guest some soda or coffee. With a nonalcoholic drink, the patron probably won't feel so embarrassed at being shut off. If the customer appears dangerously drunk, quietly offer to call a cab. Some people will appreciate your kindness and sensitivity . . . some will call you names you've never heard of before. If a patron sets off fireworks at the suggestion of a shut-off, you may have to become more forceful; summon the manager to help you, and, if necessary, the police as well. Despite the hassle it might cause you at the time, your responsible, alert attitude towards intoxicated people will probably spare everybody much greater problems later.

If you're the creative type, you might scoff at such boring suggestions. Use your imagination (careful, though!) in throwing out drunks—don't always rely on a discreet soda water or a burly, bicep-bound bouncer to help you out of these situations. Tom, a graduate of the Harvard Bartending Course, keeps control of every problem with his special weapon: a sense of humor. He works in a busy, crowded bar situated in the center of town, so he can't easily keep count of how many drinks each patron has already had, either in his bar or at nearby bars earlier in the day. One night, a particularly sloshed patron dropped by after having spent the afternoon at the pub next door. This customer stumbled up to the bar and tried desperately to focus his eyes and unglue his tongue from the top of his mouth to order a drink. As the drunk attempted to steady himself on the edge of a stool, Tom quipped, "Buddy, I hope you're driving home—you'll never make it walking." The customer got quite a chuckle out of that one, and agreed with Tom's decision to shut him off. (Tom thinks "agreed" might be the wrong word. He feels perhaps the customer really had no idea what was going on around him.)

Amy, another Harvard Bartending grad, agrees with Tom's philosophy. "Many people who have drunk too much feel pretty jolly, and will respond more readily to a friendly, lighthearted bartender. Nobody likes to be sternly reprimanded or treated like a child." With that in mind, Amy takes a rather cheerful approach to refusing service. If a customer orders a "Schcotch and shoda," she smiles and promises, "When you learn how to say it, the drink's on the house," as she plunks down a glass of water on the bar and walks away. Later, she'll come back and quietly offer to call a cab, but she tries to make light of the whole matter to help the customer feel more comfortable. Many patrons even return the next night, order the drink again (this time, "Scotch and soda"), and receive their free reward. Sure, a remark like that might get you in trouble with the wrong customer, but Amy rarely has any problems.

Of the Harvard Bartending grads we talked to, MaryLee follows the strictest guidelines. "If one of my customers tried to drive home drunk and ended up killing someone, I couldn't live with myself . . . I'd feel like a murderer." Motivated by this fear, MaryLee absolutely refuses to serve liquor to a drunk, and she does it in a very straightforward manner. She immediately calls a bouncer over who then hustles the drinker out of the bar and into a cab. She's seen several customers put up a struggle and has been called many nasty names, but none of MaryLee's patrons has ever had an accident.

Minors pose another problem. You probably know the legal

drinking age in your state, so do *not* serve alcohol to minors.
Ask for positive identification from all suspected teens and
refuse service if they cannot produce it. If caught serving
underage people, a bar might automatically have its license
suspended or revoked and be forced to pay hefty fines.

Luke has tended bar for four years since receiving his
Harvard Master of Mixology degree. "I don't take any
chances. If I find *any* reason to suspect someone is underage,
I throw the kid out. Sometimes I even get the manager just to
scare them a little." Luke claims he knows every trick now—
sisters' and brothers' IDs, duplicate licenses with the right
picture but the wrong name, excuses like "But I left my
license in my other wallet," fake mail-order IDs, school IDs
with no date ("That code number there under my picture
means I'm twenty"), and countless other ploys. Luke also

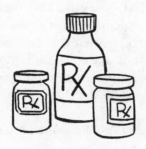

tries to keep an eye out for minors who convince older people to buy drinks for them. "I like my job. This is a great bar. I'm not about to ruin everything just for some punk who wants a drink."

Tom, Amy, MaryLee, and Luke exemplify the Harvard Bartender: they're responsible, alert, and know that bartending doesn't begin and end with just mixing drinks. They are aware of the side effects alcohol may elicit in drinkers, and consider such knowledge part of the job. As Luke says, "A pharmacist wouldn't dispense drugs he didn't understand the effects of—neither will I."

:7:

Helping Those Who Can't Help Themselves
Professional Bartending

C lose your eyes. Now, think . . . think way back, a
long, long time ago . . . no, think further
back—before you read chapter 1 . . . Aaah, do you remember
now? Yes, *you* were once a Problem Drinkmaker. Of course,
it's easy to look back on those days now and laugh, but
remember—the thousands of lonely, confused, thirsty
Problem Drinkmakers out there in the world today *need your
help*. Those wretched souls can't mix their own drinks. They
probably don't even know the first thing about bartending,
believe it or not. So, ex–Problem Drinkmaker, *you* must pour
for them.

What? Certainly you're not afraid to become a professional
bartender, are you? Well, just in case you're still a little bit
shaky on the idea of going pro, the Harvard Bartending
Course presents its time-tested and coveted hints on how to
use your new bartending skills as a professional, including:

● Looking for a job
● Appearance: It's more than just showing up
● Attitude: How to keep your customers and managers
  happy—at the same time!

Looking for a Job

In many bars, a high employee turnover makes bartending an ideal job to break into. If you hit the right place at the right time, *presto*—you've got a job.

Well, maybe not quite "presto." In fact, we sort of . . . um . . . lied to you throughout the book. Whoa, don't get upset! Let us explain. Remember reading how easy bartending is? Remember how we explained each drink-mixing process as though a two-year-old child could do it? Well, when you start dealing with professionals in real bars, it's not quite that simple. (Two-year-olds have to wait at least sixteen years to tend bar in most states.) But don't worry. We're here to make the pro scene as simple and painless as possible for you.

The hard part is that working in a fancy bar requires *speed, efficiency,* and *experience*—three skills you cannot acquire from merely reading a book or taking a course. That's where we fibbed to you. No matter how many times you carefully read chapter 2 or how many drink recipes you diligently memorized in chapter 3, you will not be able to stroll into the Ritz tomorrow and land a job. You'll have to start at the bottom and work your way up.

Now for the good news: The bottom of the bartending world isn't necessarily the worst place in the world. You don't have to start out in a miserable spot where the boss harasses you and the customers run you ragged. Rather, "bottom" generally refers to places where you won't make much money; the low salaries, poor customers, and empty barrooms won't pay your rent. Compensation for hard work at the bottom comes in the form of the speed, efficiency, and experience you will gain so you can move up to the next, higher-paying tier.

Janet, a graduate of the Harvard Bartending Course, began her brilliant career at a small, personal corner bar. She highly recommends a similar initiation for other recently reformed Problem Drinkmakers. At these small places, beginners acquire speed, efficiency, and experience in a friendly, uncrowded, low-pressure atmosphere. Jan especially enjoyed the bond shared with regular customers: "They were all so helpful and kind, even at first when I made terrible, embarrassing mistakes. . . . I knew all the regulars by name and favorite drink by the end of the first week." Although she now works in a new high-paying job, Janet often returns to her old bar to have a drink with customers—and to give her replacement a few friendly hints.

Although this suggestion may seem to contradict the last, very large bars are also excellent places to find that first job. They often have such a large employee pool and high turnover rate that they hire frequently and will settle for an inexperienced bartender. If the advantage of a small bar is its friendly, uncrowded, low-pressure environment, the advantage of a large bar is just the opposite. Sure, you'd be just one more anonymous bartender, probably at a huge bar serving hoardes of thirsty, pushy strangers, but as Richard discovered, that situation is great for a beginner. With the ink still wet on his Harvard Master of Mixology diploma, Richard donned his favorite, snazziest dancing clothes and boogied into a downtown discothèque. The manager, impressed by the diploma, hired Richard for a busy 25-person shift. Rich loved it. First of all, whenever the bar got crowded, some of his 24 skilled co-workers worked faster until the crowd thinned out; Richard just poured at his own pace. Second, Richard became a better bartender in a shorter time than many of his classmates because he worked under the pressure of all those pushy customers. Third, obscured in anonymity, Rich felt very comfortable. He didn't have to worry as much if he made mistakes at first, or forgot exactly how a regular customer liked his drink. Fourth, and most important to Richard, "I'm a stuffy accountant by day and a bartender by night. All day I look forward to coming in here to be with all these people having a great time. I'd go almost as stir-crazy in a small, boring bar as I do in my small, boring office!"

Unlike Richard, when Leslie graduated from Harvard Bartending, her days as a Problem Drinkmaker felt too close for comfort. "I was terrified at the thought of all those customers— the crowds of strangers waiting impatiently, pushing each other in line and staring at me while I spilled drinks all over myself." Today, Leslie is the head bartender, manager of twenty employees, in a fancy restaurant. She cured herself of customer phobia by beginning her career in the restaurant's service bar where she dealt with only waiters and waitresses, *not* customers. This kind of bar allowed her a little more time to sort out confused thoughts and to mix each drink slowly and privately. Eventually, Leslie gained skill and confidence and requested a transfer to the restaurant lounge so she could earn more tips. The rest is history.

About the same time Leslie went into hiding at a secluded service bar, her classmate Herman set out to find his first job. Unlike Leslie, Herman dreamed of bartending stardom. He envisioned throngs of adoring fans flocking to his bar, gazing in wonder and admiration at his every stunningly graceful move as he dazzled them with bartending brilliance. Unfortunately, Herm was more of a performer than a student—the only drink recipes he remembered were gin and tonics, vodka and tonics, Scotch and sodas, and El Presidente Herminio (his favorite).

Furthermore, with a mind like that, he obviously faced some difficulty handling money in a crowded bar. Undaunted, Herman looked in the Yellow Pages for catering services, applied to several, called them a few weeks later to reapply, and finally found a job. The catering agency sent him to cocktail parties, weddings, and other private functions where he learned the basics while "performing" for hundreds of guests. The agency billed each account, so Herman never had to assume responsibility for money. What does Herman like best about his job? "The father of the bride. You can't imagine what this tearful man will shell out in tip money after his baby just left for her honeymoon—and he's had a few Scotch and waters."

When Maura and Hope graduated from Harvard Bartending, both pounded the pavement for two weeks to find their first jobs. In fact, they kept right on pounding, even after the second, third, and fourth jobs—drumming up business for their very own bartending service. "We noticed many party hosts and hostesses have absolutely no idea where to turn when they need a bartender," Maura explained, "so we just took advantage of their ignorance and went to them first." To get their bartending business off the ground, Maura and Hope put ads in the newspapers, distributed flyers announcing their services, left eye-catching business cards in office buildings and at the cash registers in liquor stores and bridal shops, and told everyone they knew to spread the word around town. After working several successful jobs, the pair discovered that word-of-mouth gave the business momentum to keep it going.

College communities require the services of many bartenders. If you are a student and your school does not have a student catering/bartending agency, check with the administration about how you can start one up yourself. Or, for the more moderately ambitious, just post flyers around campus advertising your services. Put an ad in the school paper. Let people know you're available and you'll be stirring martinis for your professors in no time.

If you decide to sell yourself as a bartender, check local

catering agencies and bar employees to see how much they charge for their services. Make sure your prices are competitive before trying to break into the business. Also, if you haven't already done so, read chapter 4 so you'll be able to run your bartending service with class and experience.

In some cities, you could start your bartending career by joining the Hotel and Restaurant, Institutional Employees and Bartenders Union. Large hotels, restaurant chains, and other unionized establishments sometimes hire directly through the union, so membership will spare you the tedious door-knocking you'll have to do otherwise. Harvard Bartending graduates cannot follow this route to break into bartending because the Boston local does not provide a job referral service, instead serving primarily as an organization for employed bartenders. If interested, you should call the union in your area to inquire about job referral opportunities.

To land *your* first job, whether in a big bar or small, be prepared for a tedious, often discouraging, job search. Don't despair if the first manager you speak to—or the second or third—doesn't hire you on the spot.

Be persistent. Speak politely to each manager, emphasizing how hard you will work and how willing you are to accept low pay to gain the experience. Stress your superb educational background—proudly display that Harvard Bartending Course diploma. (Diploma information is at the back of the book.) Eventually, your perseverance, charm, and knowledge are bound to impress somebody.

After working at one of these places for a while, you'll feel like a pro behind the bar, will have acquired speed and efficiency, and will be able to provide a reference to your next potential employer when you move up to a better-paying, more desirable job.

Appearance

Everyone knows a bartender can't just show up for a job, pour drinks efficiently, and then go home with a pocketful of tips and a glowing recommendation from the boss. A bartender has to learn how to please the customers and the managers—at the same time.

A clean, spiffy appearance is crucial for professional bartending. In a restaurant, the manager can hide a grubby, slovenly cook back in the kitchen if he has to. By contrast, bartenders work right up front, handling ice and fruit in full view of the critical customers. Obviously, a good bartender must look immaculate and well-groomed; drinks prepared by a sloppy bartender with dirty hands are unappealing, to say the least— who knows what's in them? Of course, if you choose to work at Sleazy Sam's Saloon where the customers consist of Hell's Angels, winos, stray cats, and a large family of cockroaches, then you can look like whatever you want.

Regarding clothing, most bar managers will tell you what to wear when they hire you and will request that you wear clothes appropriate for the bar's style. Whatever you wear, always look neat and comfortable so you can maintain a cool, confident bartender image, even after several hectic hours. If you're allowed to choose your dress in a somewhat fancy place or a catering agency, or if you're self-employed, stick with traditional bar attire. Men wear dark pants and shoes with a white shirt and a bow tie. The bow tie idea might sound silly, but picture yourself in a long tie, leaning over to serve a drink to a customer, and *splat*—the tip of your tie dives into the drink. Surely not to insinuate that you're clumsy—but a bowtie will make life easier by giving you the freedom of movement a busy bartender needs. Women should wear a dark skirt or slacks and shoes with a white blouse. Tie long hair back neatly, for the same reason a bow tie is recommended for men.

Try to keep your appearance behind the bar as close to neutral as possible. A good bartender is like good vodka—he or she promotes a pleasant feeling, but remains essentially neutral and blends easily into many surroundings. Both men and women should avoid wearing flashy jewelry, political buttons, and outrageous clothing. If you have any doubts as to the neutral-ity of a hair style or article of clothing, do not wear it. Some bars may promote an off-beat appearance, but most prefer the more conservative look. Use your own judgment in these matters, but remember—although customers probably won't speak up and tell you when your appearance has offended them, their tips will.

Attitude and Behavior

Or: How to Keep the Customers and Bar Managers Thrilled with You—at the Same Time! In a way, this aspect of bartending is more important than anything else. You can make a few mistakes mixing drinks and nobody notices. But just try making a mistake pleasing a customer, and the whole bar hears about it.

Whatever may happen, look like you know what you're doing. Nine times out of ten, a confident attitude will fool the customer, even if you have no idea what goes in a rum and Coke. If you maintain that image of authority, patrons won't question your ability to mix a drink or your decision to shut off a a drunk. Customers and bar managers get uncomfortable when they see their bartender stumbling around, looking confused, or scowling and muttering irritably. Always smile (or at least look cocky), grab bottles by the neck surely and swiftly, speak clearly and positively, and act like you know every drink ever invented.

Wait—that last word of wisdom needs a bit of clarification. Don't feel mortified if you must ask the customer what goes in a drink. Perhaps you should blush if you don't know the ingredients in a gin and tonic, but nobody expects you to remember El

Presidente Herminio or Jump-Up-and-Kiss-Me. Don't be afraid to ask, and don't rule out the possibility of bluffing a bit since the customer probably doesn't even know the ingredients of the really exotic drinks. Why embarrass him or her by asking? Chris, the venerable instructor of the Harvard Bartending Course, tells students, "If your bluff is called, you can always talk your way out of it." Once, when Chris was just beginning his illustrious career, a customer ordered a Hop-Skip-and-Go-Naked. Chris vaguely remembered that the drink must be pretty strong to merit such a name, so he confidently sauntered to the back bar, threw in a little of this, a dash of that, a few ounces of six flavored brandies, some coloring, several rums, and five different garnishes. He presented the masterpiece with a flourish to the customer, who stared at the concoction in horror and protested, "But that's not one ounce vodka, one ounce gin, and the juice from half a lime, filled with beer!" Chris, thinking quickly (as usual), replied, "Oh, you wanted a *Western* Hop-Skip-and-Go-Naked. I made you the *Eastern* version!"

You might also need to use that story in all honesty some day. Many drinks change drastically from one region of the country to another or even one bar to another. Just try to keep on top of variations as much as possible, and *act confident*.

THE CUSTOMER (aarghh!) IS ALWAYS RIGHT

However painful it may be to see this paradoxical axiom in practice, the customer *is* always right. If a patron accuses you of making a drink wrong, at least go through the motions of altering it according to his or her wishes. Sometimes a difficult customer has had a hard day or just wants a little more attention. Don't ever say, "No, you're wrong. I learned the correct way to make the drink in my *Harvard Student Agencies Bartending Course*." Nobody ever got rich on an obnoxious statement like that.

The moment an almighty customer arrives, you should

spring into action: smile, greet the guest warmly, and drop whatever you were doing to wait on him or her. Try to remember the faces (names, if introduced) and tastes of your regular customers so you can offer "the usual" as soon as they come in.

Always treat customers courteously. Never hurry them or show irritation. Whenever you feel the urge to become impatient, conjure up the image of a huge padlock clamping shut on the customer's wallet. If that doesn't soothe your frazzled temper, nothing will.

Be aware of whom you talk to and when. Never appear to be listening in on a conversation or trying to take part. As soon as you have served a drink, step back from the customer or move away. Some folks will want to talk to you . . . desperately. You'll find out quickly about those lonely types. On the other hand, a couple having a personal argument doesn't want to hear your opinion on the matter, so butt out. If invited to chat with someone for a moment, never talk about another customer or gossip about scandals you've witnessed at the bar—including your own; it's safer and more professional to leave your personal life at home.

If you must answer a telephone at the bar, do so quietly. If the call is for a patron, *never* say the person is there. Instead, offer to inquire, and leave it up to the customer to decide whether to answer the phone.

To help you think of more ways to extract tips from a patron, put yourself in the customer's seat for a minute and look at the bartender's job from the other side of the bar.

Don't you love to be pampered? Doesn't everybody? Aren't you just tickled when a bartender drops everything to light your cigarette? Aren't you pleased when a careful bartender cares enough to empty the ashtray correctly? (He or she puts a clean ashtray over the dirty one and lifts both from the bar—to avoid blowing ashes all over the place—and then places the clean tray on the bar). Don't you feel sort of special when a bartender spends extra time pouring the first glass from the bottle of beer—and gets just the right amount of foam on top? And then don't you reach for your wallet to show your gratitude . . . ?

YES, BOSS. RIGHT AWAY, M'AM.
ANYTHING YOU SAY, SIR.

Bartenders who offend customers just lose their tips. Bartenders who offend the boss lose their jobs. (Although one way to offend the boss is to offend the customers.) Managers expect all bartenders, even beginners, to adhere to a set of common-sense guidelines. Therefore, if you want to keep your job, get raises, work better shifts, and earn a flattering job reference, you'd best impress the boss.

Managers and customers think highly of a busy, hard-working bartender. Even during a lull period, you can always find plenty to do around the bar: wipe spills, wash glasses, clean ashtrays, cut fruit, make pre-mixes (such as sour mix and Bloody Mary mix) and pick up dirty glasses, straws, and napkins. Even when you talk to customers, look busy and you'll make a good impression on everybody.

If you don't hit that lull period, take a few seconds here and there to keep the bar clean. Customers won't want to drink at a messy, littered bar, so managers always frown upon a slob behind the bar.

If you're looking for the quickest, easiest way to get fired, try cheating on your boss. Bar managers have worked in the business for a long time and can tell when a bartender takes a few dollars here and there or serves free drinks to friends.

In fact, managers even notice when a bartender has a heavy hand with liquor bottles. If inventories fall especially low after a certain bartender's shift, that person has poured too much into each drink. Be stingy! Also be thrifty regarding which brands you use. In most operations, you'll be told to put the cheapest ("house" or "bar") brand in a drink unless the customer requests a "call" (name) brand.

If the manager doesn't catch you cheating right away and you're becoming antsy for unemployment, have a few drinks. Drinking on the job makes you an inefficient bartender and proves you have no respect for the boss or the customers. All you have to do is spill a drink, slur a few words, and insult a customer—before you can even hiccup, you'll be out in the street.

As you shower your boss with attentions, don't ignore co-workers. Treat them with courtesy, too. Make sure to leave the bar clean, orderly, and well stocked with supplies at the end of your shift. If someone asks you to fill in for a shift, do so whenever possible. Of course, co-workers can't fire you for an unpleasant disposition, but bar work is much more fun when employees get along well and help each other.

Pass the Bucks

Proficiency in money handling requires practice. In a busy bar, many errors result from giving change for the wrong amount of money, such as when a bartender mistakes a ten-dollar bill for a twenty. To minimize these errors, follow the process of the "5 Cs": collect cash; call it; cash register; correct till-slot; count change back.

1. *Collect cash:* So you don't forget in the confusion of a busy bar, collect the money for a drink right after you serve it. (If your bar has a tab or check system, the manager will teach you the correct procedure to follow.)

2. *Call it:* "Call" the amount of money. When the customer hands you the bill, say "That's two-fifty out of ten." You'll be more likely to remember exactly what you have.

3. *Cash register:* Keep the bill on top of the cash register until you hand the customer the change. You will remember what amount to make change from, and will be protected if the customer insists, "But I gave you a twenty-dollar bill, not a ten."

4. *Correct till-slot:* Get in the habit of putting each

denomination in the correct till-slot of the cash register. Then, if the customer says you counted the change wrong, check the register to see if you put the bill in the wrong slot.

5. *Count change back:* Count the change back to the customer, saying, "two-fifty out of ten: Here's fifty cents for three dollars, two more to make five, and five more makes ten," as you hand back the money.

If you cannot satisfactorily handle a customer complaint, call the manager. Usually, money complications become the manager's responsibility. Don't be insulted, however, if the manager returns the customer's money without question—remember, the customer is always right. If a similar problem occurs involving the same customer a second time, you and the manager should proceed cautiously. You're probably being cheated.

You will also have to handle tip money in a bar. Some places pool all the tips earned in a given shift and then split the money equally among all the bartenders. This method is equitable when bartenders share areas and, therefore, customers.

Never announce the amount of a tip, no matter how great or small. It's embarrassing to the customer, and incredibly tacky.

BUT OSSIFER, I FEEL WONNERFUL . . .

Protect yourself and your employer. *Read chapter 6.* With the recent nationwide crackdown on drunk driving, bartenders and managers must assume more responsibility for the people they serve—or face legal consequences.

Once you get working, you'll find hundreds of ways to delight and amuse the Problem Drinkmaker. For example, the latest addition to the Harvard Bartending Course is a magic lesson, offering students the option of learning a few magic tricks to entertain and, of course, pull tips from their customers. Now don't get all excited and think chapter 8 is all about magic tricks—even we're not crazy enough to try to teach magic in print. Use your imagination. As a recently reformed Problem Drinkmaker, think back to the days when you sat on the customer's stool—what did you like?

When all else fails, and you've just served seventeen nasty people in a row, broken a tray of glasses, and spilled a whole

drink on yourself, *laugh*. You've got to prepare yourself for some unpleasant occurences during your professional bartending career, so learn now not to take yourself too seriously. On the whole, bartending should be fun, lively and interesting. If not, have you considered a career as an actuary or perhaps a garbage collector?

:8:

The Bar Exam
Are You Really *Cured?*

I f you've read even a few pages of this book and have tried some recipes on your friends, you've already learned a good deal about bartending. But are you *really* cured of Problem Drinkmaking? Take this Bar Exam to be sure. Circle the correct answers, tally up your score, tear out the exam, and mail it to the Harvard Bartending Course to receive your official diploma (see page 205). Good luck, and may the Course be with you.

1. A gin chiller is:
   a. frozen Beefeaters
   b. gin, ginger ale, and a lime wedge
   c. a little funny animal that they make fur coats out of

2. An extra-dry martini . . .
   a. . . . contains very little vermouth
   b. . . . is just a glass full of olives
   c. . . . will not spill

3. A fifth is:
   a. the drink you have after your fourth
   b. 5 ounces of five-star brandy with a twist
   c. 1/5 gallon or 4/5 quart

4. A Manhattan is:
   a. one part New York State wine, one part ginger ale
   b. four parts bourbon, one part sweet vermouth
   c. one part Black & White, a dash of Puerto Rican rum, and a splash of Chinese wine

5. An Angel's Kiss is:
   a. what you get when you drink and drive
   b. 1 oz. Cherubim, 1 oz. crème de seraphim, 1 oz. liqueur de nuages, shaken, strained into a Hershey glass
   c. ¼ brandy, ¼ cream, ¼ Crème Yvette, ¼ crème de cacao

6. A Godfather is:
   a. a cocktail you can't refuse
   b. 1½ oz. bourbon or blended, ½ oz. amaretto
   c. 1 part four-star brandy, 3 parts Marlon Brandy, shaken well and served over crushed ice in a broken glass

7. A one-man bar is best suited for:
   a. parties of 15 to 100 people
   b. people who like to drink alone
   c. shy bartenders

8. If you will be bartending at a party for senior citizens, and the hostess asks you for advice in liquor selection, you should suggest:
   a. serve only Old Fashioneds
   b. spike the punch with Geritol
   c. order more dark alcohol

9. "Mist" refers to:
   a. when a Problem Drinkmaker tries to pour a drink into the glass but instead spills it all over the bar. . . . "Oops, I mist!"

    b. a liqueur served over shaved ice
    c. the fog surrounding a hangover victim's head

10. A Presbyterian is made of:
    a. hell-fire and ginger ale
    b. brimstone and bourbon
    c. whiskey, ginger ale, and soda
    d. Nonalcoholic ingredients

11. A dry Manhattan is:
    a. New York, 1920–1933.
    b. New York, four A.M. to six A.M.
    c. A regular Manhattan, but with dry vermouth instead
       of sweet
    d. A Manhattan that never spills

: Exam Answer Key :

11.	C	(see page 47)
10.	C	(see page 37)
9.	B	(see page 18)
8.	C	(see page 100)
7.	A	(see page 108)
6.	B	(see page 51)
5.	C	(see page 87)
4.	B	(see page 47)
3.	C	(see page 17)
2.	A	(see page 46)
1.	B	(see page 32)

Scoring:

    Give yourself 1 point for each right answer. Subtract 500 points for each wrong answer.

    If you scored a positive number, you *passed!* If you scored a negative number, you passed out—only an unconscious person could get these wrong.

:9:

Graduation

How to order your very own Bartending Kit, T-shirt, and official Harvard Bartending Correspondence Course diploma

Did you pass the bar exam? Maybe got just one question wrong, but erased your answer so we won't notice? Congratulations! You're cured!

Stop for a moment and think about what this really means. No more Problem Drinkmaking. No more embarrassment. Never again will you blush and stammer at cocktail parties, trying desperately to hide your crippling defect from family and friends. Never again will you be forced to drink beer and wine all night at a bar, too ignorant to order even a gin and tonic, much less a Tom and Jerry. Gone are the days when you kissed your thirsty date good-bye at the door, unable to risk inviting him or her in for a nightcap.

Don't let this momentous occasion slip by without fanfare. On the next page, you'll find out how to graduate from The

Official Harvard Student Agencies Bartending Course in style. Fill out that order form right away, drop it in the nearest mailbox, and then call all your friends to go out and celebrate—with *real* drinks—your new identity.

Welcome to the real world.

Cheers!

GET HELP BY MAIL . . .

A. BARTENDING KIT

Comes with everything you need to be a successful bartender! Shaker, mixing glass, strainer, bar spoon, jigger/pony, corkscrew, and six speedpourers. $25.00

B. EXTRA SPEEDPOURERS

For your expanding bar needs. Package of six. $3.25

C. GIFT CERTIFICATE

Send help to a Problem Drinkmaker friend in New England -- a certificate good for one admission to the original Harvard Bartending Course. This lively, three-night course run by Harvard Student Agencies, Inc., meets biweekly on the Harvard Campus. Professional instructors lead Problem Drinkmakers through an entertaining, comprehensive introduction to mixology which culminates in "lab night," where students prepare and taste a variety of drinks. Order today -- don't make that friend suffer any longer! $40.00

D. DIPLOMA

If you've successfully completed the Harvard Bartending Correspondence Course, congratulations! Send us your Bar Exam and you'll receive a Master of Mixology Diploma, suitable for framing. $5.00

(note: prices valid through 9/30/90)

ORDER FORM

ITEM	QTY	AMOUNT
A. BARTENDING KIT: $25.00 plus $2.00 postage & handling. (Mass. residents add 5% sales tax.)	___	_____
B. EXTRA SPEEDPOURERS: $3.25 (Mass. residents add 5% sales tax.)	___	_____
C. GIFT CERTIFICATE: $40.00	___	_____
D. DIPLOMA: $5.00 plus $2.00 postage & handling.	___	_____

Name _____

Address (no. & street) _____

City/State/Zip _____

Telephone ( ) _____

Enclose a check or
money order payable to:

HARVARD STUDENT AGENCIES, INC.
Thayer Hall-B
Harvard University
Cambridge, Ma. 02138
(617) 495-9657

TOTAL: _____

LET'S GO

Harvard Student Agencies, Inc.

"No other guides give quite as much...the sheer wealth of information in these guides makes them well worth the price."

—U.P.I.

The *LET'S GO* series is:
- Updated every year
- Researched and written just months before press time

- Hundreds of new pages of travel information
- Backed by more researchers than ever before

The Budget Guide for Student Travelers

Available at bookstores, or use coupon provided.

Index

DO YOU KNOW A PROBLEM DRINKMAKER?

Sometimes it's hard to tell people—even your closest friends—that something's wrong with them.

Well, we can help. Additional copies of this book can be ordered through your local bookstore.

Or, if you just can't face walking up to that certain someone and saying, "You're a Problem Drinkmaker," let us do it for you. Just fill out the coupon below and mail it with your payment to St. Martin's Press. Within six weeks, your friend will get the message: his or her very own copy of *The Official Harvard Student Agencies Bartending Course*, mailed in a plain brown wrapper (well, almost).

It's a gift that keeps on giving.

ORDER FORM

Please send _____ copies of *The Official Harvard Student Agencies Bartending Course* @ $5.95 each. Please enclose $1.25 for postage and handling for the first copy and $.50 for each additional copy. Send check or money order to: St. Martin's Press, Cash Sales Dept., 175 Fifth Avenue, New York, N.Y. 10010.

Name _____

Address _____

City _____

State _____ Zip _____